HAMLET'S MIRROR

Reaching Your Performance Potential Onstage and Off

ELMA LINZ KANEFIELD, LCSW
with DIANNE CONJEAUD

For permission requests, contact the publisher at the website below
Elma Linz Kanefield, LCSW, PLLC
www.elmalinzkanefield.com

Library of Congress Control Number: 2022909404
Paperback ISBN: 979-8-9862605-0-1
Printed in the United States of America

Interior Design: KUHN Design Group

DEDICATION:

Howard Kanefield, my husband, the wind beneath my wings.

Norman Pearlstein, my muse since he was ten and I was thirteen.

CONTENTS

PROLOGUE

Hamlet's Mirror is the culmination of all I've seen and learned over the last thirty-five years as a specialist in the psychology of the performing artist.

Over the years, I have come to understand that the essence of my work is empowering performers to realize both their personal and professional performance potential.

Performance potential strikes a different chord for every performer.

In one of my master classes, I asked a singer what performance potential meant to him.

"That's a very personal question," he replied.

Indeed, it is. But when a different singer was asked the same question, she responded with great emotion: "It's that possibility I have inside."

In my office I have a ballet barre. A dancer went to the barre and extended her leg. With the grace of her entire body, she told me her performance potential was her stretch, her reach.

A young actor said: "It's what my parents have told me I'm not living up to."

Responses to my question run the gamut from "It's the special greatness I hold within," to "You're asking me something I've never even dared to say out loud."

A musician defined performance potential as *doing*.

I agree.

I define performance potential as being the best you can be and doing the best you can do based on what you know in the moment of performance.

PERFORMANCE POTENTIAL

**Being the best you can be and doing the best you can do
based on what you know in the moment of performance.**

I am often asked why I work exclusively with performers. I believe my work as a psychotherapist and life coach has many aspects in common with the performing arts. Both seek to uncover the truth and meaning, the mysteries and myths of the human condition. Both use curiosity, creativity and imagination as fundamental instruments of discovery. Whether through memory, cognition and emotional experience, or through music, movement, vision, and dialogue, both my work and the performing arts seek to understand what drives human beings to be motivated, aroused and inspired, or the contrary. Each is live and interactive. Each requires training, discipline, empathy and experience. Both are powerful. Each is transformative.

As a clinician I've had the opportunity to look into the eyes of performers who sing, dance and make music eight times a week, in ensemble, corps and background work, who approach each performance as if it's the very first time. I've sat across from artists whose music, dance or drama, on stage, screen and television, marks important events in our lives, gives us a sense of hope, makes us feel alive, and those to whom many of us are grateful for sheltering our very souls.

Interacting with them in this way has been more rewarding than I could ever begin to express. I've journeyed to the inner worlds of artists who inspire, give goose bumps, and whose fame or infamy generate endless hours of conversation. I've worked with artists who draw crowds in the thousands as well as those who cradle us to sleep at night, and of course, others who play with our emotions in ways we can hardly tolerate.

Because of this unique experience, I've accumulated incomparable insight and awareness about performing artists from all ages and stages of their careers. In *Hamlet's Mirror,* I am able to give them a vision of themselves they've never seen.

In these pages, I look at the culture of the performing artist and also introduce four Performer Personality Profiles.

My understanding of the culture of the performing artist has been informed by the voices of these artists. Like all other cultures, the culture of the performing artist has its own population, institutions, set of shared values, knowledge, collective rituals, accomplishments, occupational hurdles, professional hardships, and psychological hazards. Their culture is not divorced from mainstream culture and is shaped by societal norms such as freedom of expression and pressures including racism and sexism.

From these many discussions about culture, lifestyle, as well as other more personal dialogues, I've identified and classified four Performer Personality Profiles: The Problem-Ridden Performer, The Pugnacious Performer, The Promising Performer, and the Potential-Realized Performer. I also introduce the concept of energy. As I define it in my work, energy forms the foundation of the four performer personality profiles.

Throughout the text, I offer stories about performers with whom I've worked. I call these Tableaux. These Tableaux are used to illustrate specific concepts. To maintain and respect the confidentiality of the performers, I've woven their stories and identities into composite characters to whom I've given fictional names, save one.

HOLDING *HAMLET'S MIRROR*

What made you buy this book?
Are you reflecting on this question?

> **Reflection:** (n.) the contemplation of a subject matter, idea or purpose; an interactive practice. (v.) to think and/or feel deeply about.

Hamlet's Mirror is an interactive book.

In the performing arts, directors give notes, choreographers give notes, conductors give notes. These are mine. I call them Notable Reflections.

Notable Reflections are self-reflective questions which enhance the concepts that will be explored throughout the book. They are one of the primary interactive features of *Hamlet's Mirror* and enable you to measure various dimensions of your performance potential. When you regularly practice your *Notable Reflections*, you will have an opportunity to learn and change based on your responses.

As you are reading *Hamlet's Mirror*, you can take note about what you've just read, take a moment to contemplate how each *Reflection* is relevant to you and your life. At the end of each, you will be asked, WHAT ARE YOU SEEING? You will always have a response. Even when you think that a particular *Reflection* might not apply to you, that insight itself is a new way of looking at things.

REFLECTION 1

Performance Potential

Performance Potential is dynamic.

How much are you currently reaching your performance potential?

1 —— 2 —— 3 —— 4 —— 5 —— 6 —— 7 —— 8

1 being the lowest and 8 being the highest.

WHAT ARE YOU SEEING?

Hamlet's Mirror is my thank you note to the hundreds of actors, dancers, musicians and vocal artists with whom I've worked. And, although this book is about these performers, I was not surprised to discover that the insights and wisdom gained from them are relevant and applicable to us all and can empower everyone to reach their performance potential.

As you hold the mirror, I hope you'll thank them too.

"It is our artists after all who hold a mirror up to life…"

SING

TABLEAU ONE:
THE YOUNG WOMAN, TAKE ONE

The Young Woman stepped out from the wings onto a small New York stage and into the cone of light shining down just for her. Trying desperately to ignore the sounds of wrestling papers and shifting bodies in creaking chairs, she took a deep breath. The whirling voices in her head were more difficult to discount: "Will they like me? Do I look all right? I hope I hit that note."

Seconds felt like hours. She closed her eyes, rocked her head slowly and gently tapped out the rhythm of her slightly under-rehearsed medley as the first notes of her music reached her. She took another deep breath, held it, then slowly exhaled while lifting her chin, focusing on the exit light at the back of the performance hall.

The Young Woman opened her beautifully painted mouth to produce… silence.

The Young Woman was me.

My stage name was Elma Linz, and my dream since childhood was to live in New York City, attend The Juilliard School, and sing at The Metropolitan Opera. I had perfect pitch, a great ear and a natural ability to interpret music. I could sing anything from opera to blues, and I did.

At the age of eighteen I had moved to Manhattan to attend The Neighborhood Playhouse, where I studied with renowned drama teacher Sandy Meisner; and outside the Playhouse, with the great voice teacher Estelle Libeling. I also performed in several New York off-Broadway productions and did summer stock. I thought I had died and gone to heaven.

Of course, I was not exempt from the nastier aspects of show business. When I first auditioned for the Playhouse in New York, the director said, "Elma, your last name is too Jewish to go up in lights. You want to be marketable." I was so eager to please that I was willing to give up a part of myself to be up on that stage. I dropped my "too-Jewish" name and took my middle name: Elma Linz.

The first few months at there, I would walk into the bathroom where the students—children of very notable celebrities—would gather, and immediately their conversations would stop. Two of them initially rejected me as their scene partner. I felt like an alien, a non-New Yorker who would never fit in. I was humiliated, my shaky confidence shattered.

Later that year, my audition for *Gypsy* gave "Let Me Entertain You" a new meaning, as I was confronted with the casting couch during a callback. All the casting director wanted to do was use me. I floated away from my body. I never told a soul. On many levels, I was convinced I was just not good enough.

But on the whole, I simply adored performing—until that fateful night, when my world crumbled around me, the night I literally lost my voice. After that night, I was unable to phonate and would hyperventilate any time I tried to sing. I went to numerous voice teachers to try to understand why nothing would come out. I was nineteen years old. I saw doctors to find out if I had nodes or even worse. Each time I was given a clean bill of health. No one offered anything that worked for me. And I became totally frantic.

Shortly after that night, I met a very nice and talented young man from my hometown. I left the Playhouse, I left New York and returned to the Midwest to marry him. I tried some singing, but that one night haunted me.

I began seeing a psychiatrist who diagnosed me with an "adjustment reaction." He said all I had to do was settle into my life. Accommodate myself. Just adapt.

No one considered that maybe I was living the wrong life. Perhaps I was not in sync with who I was. Just maybe I was voiceless in my life, trying to be who everyone wanted me to be, to play the role everyone wanted me to play.

It took me years to realize that my stilled voice was an echo of many silences.

My voice was not only silenced onstage, but offstage as well… with my family, my friends and my community. I was out of tune with my values and my passion. I was avoiding who I really was in order to fulfill other people's expectations. Whether in audition, in performance, or in the bedroom, I was acting as if I were someone else in order to satisfy their ideas of me.

Being fueled by the energy and desires of others caused me not only to feel bad about myself; it also stifled my self-expression, personally and professionally.

I had allowed others to shape my attitudes, and to influence how I was thinking, how I was feeling, and ultimately how I was showing up in my life…

how I was performing. My energy was negative and self-defeating. I had denied and overlooked my own performance potential.

I felt overwhelmed, resentful, fearful, alone, disgraced in the eyes of others and certainly in my own.

Slowly, as I chose to take charge of my life, I began to hear my voice; and as it grew stronger and louder, I started to understand its message. My silenced voice was a symbol: *How I was performing one thing was how I was performing everything.*

I also came to understand that because I didn't acknowledge my own voice and tune into my own potential, my success as a performer was doomed from the beginning. I did not possess the emotional maturity, the mental discipline and focus, or the self-esteem necessary to have my art be anything other than self-serving. Instead of honoring Stanislavski's tenet of loving the art in myself, I loved myself in the art.

It took me some time to move forward on these crucial insights because there was no one who was passionate about, much less interested in, the psychology of the performing artist. There was no one who even thought about how performers cope in their psychologically tumultuous culture, or about the power of energy as the foundation of performing. And there was certainly no one who cared about what was preventing me from reaching my personal and professional performance potential.

In other words, there was no professional to help me understand that what caused me to lose my voice, onstage and off, was much more than the trauma I experienced as Elma Linz.

When I finally gained clarity, I enrolled in graduate school at the age of twenty-nine and became a psychotherapist to help other performing artists become aware of the effect that their personal and professional histories have on who they are, and how they show up in their lives—how their history impacts their performance potential.

At the age of forty, divorced and with two grown sons, I took my passion one step further; I closed the clinical practice I had developed in the Midwest and relocated to Manhattan. There, I thought, a private practice exclusive to the psychological well-being of performing artists was a natural. I assumed I'd be one of many clinicians in New York City— the mecca for performing artists— who did what I planned to do.

Was I ever wrong! To my knowledge, nobody else had a clinical practice focused solely on the psychology of the performing artist.

Dreams… I had transformed my silenced voice into my true calling, reaching my own performance potential.

In 1983, I opened my office on the Upper West Side of Manhattan, in the heart of Lincoln Center, one of the world's greatest performance sites. I also married the love of my life, Howard Kanefield. And in 1986 I answered an ad in *The New York Times* for a nine-hour, on-campus therapy position at The Juilliard School. Although I was told there were hundreds of applicants, I got the gig. What an irony that I ended up "attending" Juilliard, one way or another.

It's likely I was offered the position because I was once a performer myself, and because I had held a position at the Washington University Counseling Services in St. Louis when I first graduated from social work school there, and I had experience working with students.

I also think that those who interviewed me understood the unique nature of my New York therapy practice, and that working with performers was my passion and my life's work. I would come to Juilliard with a belief system about how to work clinically with performers, along with my own vocabulary.

Looking back, I believe that at the time of my hiring, the position at Juilliard was more of an inspiration than a practical reality: I had no office, no desk, no Julliard telephone number. I met students in various spaces throughout the building when space was available. They called my private therapy office to schedule appointments. Students being students, they would call at all hours of the day and night.

I made do. But about three months into my nine-hour-a-week position, I had heard from over sixty students and seen some severe pathology.

At this point I contacted Dr. Joseph Polisi, then president of Juilliard. The workload was not sustainable for me and there were struggling students whose needs I couldn't address.

I proposed three options. First, hospitals had been contacting me about arranging a contract that would allow students to be treated by hospital staff off-campus. Second, we could return to the old system whereby the students would talk with a wonderful psychologist, for one visit, in his private, off-campus office, free of charge. This clinician could then refer them to a colleague without follow-up.

Or, I said, Juilliard could start an on-campus counseling service.

Dr. Polisi looked me in the eye and asked, "Well, do you want to?"

I said, "Sure." However, it was a conditional agreement, as I suggested that the service be free of charge, confidential, with unlimited sessions, one new staff member and a psychiatric consultant. I also told him I believed that when hiring clinical staff to work with performing arts students, it was important that they not only be well-trained clinicians, but also that they understand the performing artists' culture, business, profession, and art forms.

Dr. Polisi looked at me once more and we shook hands. Throughout my entire tenure, Dr. Polisi honored the agreement we made that day.

I'm proud to say that The Juilliard School's Counseling Service (which grew to include a part-time staff of six, an administrative consultant, and a consulting psychiatrist) was the first of its kind: an on-campus, free-of-charge, fully staffed psychological facility offering unlimited, confidential sessions to serve the entire graduate and post-graduate student body. It continues to be the only independent performing arts school like it in the world. Bravo, Juilliard!

I thought that the Counseling Service would be important for Juilliard students—not only musicians, but also actors, dancers, and vocal artists—because I believe all performing artists are predisposed and vulnerable to mental and emotional challenges and conflicts, onstage and off. By creating the Service, I hoped to help students reach their potential as performers and as people. I continue to maintain a very close relationship with Juilliard.

In my private practice, which I maintained while at Juilliard, I have always worked exclusively with performers. My office was designed for these artists: the books on the shelves are written by or about them, the drawings on the walls are Hirschfeld's, and, much to the delight of the artists who came to see me, my four-pound poodle Brava would often grace our sessions.

Most notably, however, in my office alcove is a small stage with a piano and a ballet barre. Artists are invited not only to talk about their experiences and memories but also to reenact, in their own art forms, their personal and professional challenges and conflicts, using the stage to find transformational insights.

This is but one example of an approach that I call Psychological Coaching, combining traditional psychotherapies with a life coaching philosophy. With traditional psychological modalities, I focus on healing the past, the performer's inner world, and on reflection and contemplation. With coaching, I focus on empowerment, the here and now, both the external as well as internal worlds of the performing artist, and on accountability and action. I practice one or the other or both as needed in working with the artists I see.

With traditional psychological investigation, where the left brain is more mobilized, I use the forms of speech "why" and "how." With coaching, the right brain is more mobilized with inquiries of "who," "what," "when," and "where." The former is more analytic, the latter more creative.

Psychological Coaching involves knowledge of both the performer's personality as well as their culture. In my office, every day, I use my voice to inspire the artists with whom I work to listen carefully to theirs, to help them express it to fulfill their own performance potential onstage and off.

Elma Linz drew me to specialize in the psychology of the performing artist; Elma Linz Kanefield drew me to write *Hamlet's Mirror*.

THE CULTURE OF THE PERFORMING ARTIST

The unspoken question that I often hear in my office is, *"Does my profession nurture and protect me or does it prevent me from realizing my performance potential?"* In other words, does the culture, which revolves around me, foster and support me so that I thrive and flourish or does it disrespect, demoralize and dismiss me?

The culture of the performing artist goes back to the 6th Century BC when the Theatre of Dionysus in Athens, the birthplace of Greek Tragedy, was built. Some of the most significant ancient structures in the world are seeds of this culture. As long as these places have existed, there have been performing artists.

THE FOUR ART FORMS
DRAMA, DANCE, MUSIC AND THE VOCAL ARTS

People are often curious to know if I work more with dancers or actors, musicians or vocal artists. Over the years, it's turned out to be quite balanced. And the stories these artists have shared have allowed me to understand the personalities that each art form shapes. So, when I'm asked, *"Why are actors so histrionic, singers loud and ostentatious, dancers spacey and remote, and musicians introverted and intense?"* I'm able to respond.

I have found that there are challenges unique to each art form that fashion or amplify these stereotypes. It has proven very helpful to me to identify the specific cultural norms and demands of music, dance, drama, and voice that have created these "caricatures."

Existential Questions

As I explored further, each art form revealed its own existential question: Who Am I? What Am I? Why Am I? Where Am I? The artists with whom I've worked taught me that inherent in each of their art forms is a question that delineates how the actor, dancer, musician, and vocal artist differ from one another and the struggles they face. Each question also highlights how the art form contributes to the formation of the personality of each performing artist, and to the realization of the performer's performance potential.

Pair the performing artist - musician, dancer, vocal artist, or actor - with their existential question.

Who am I?
What am I?
Where am I?
Why am I?

Who am I: The Actor

If you paired the actor with the question *Who am I,* you understand that acting threatens the actor's identity. Actors are vulnerable to losing themselves in their roles and consequently the sense of where they begin and their character ends. Ironic—as many would-be actors enter acting to *find* themselves.

I have found that the question *Who am I?* is profoundly omnipresent in the dramatic arts. The actor's instrument is his whole being—*his body, his mind, his intuition, and his emotional life*—his tangible and intangible self. The actor's self, his identity, and his performance instrument—the tool needed to build a character—are one and the same. This union is professionally ideal and personally problematic. It creates a precarious and confusing double bind.

TABLEAU TWO: ANGELA

Angela, a beautiful stage and screen actor, could not maintain personal and professional boundaries. She found it impossible to separate her acting from her behavior offstage. She was the constant love object in her work and mirrored this by having steady affairs in her personal life. She had roles making love onscreen and love affairs off. When Angela began therapy, she was on her third marriage and about to be divorced. In spite of this, her extra-marital affairs continued because, as she explained, "I get so deep in my roles, I can't control my feelings offstage." She "made love" onscreen with so many people that it gave her unwitting permission offstage, ultimately destroying her marriages. Angela insisted that her choices and behavior did not "really" represent her as she kept asking me, "Who am I? This isn't me!"

When actors take on a role, they assume another identity, casting off their own. They must become psychologically naked. They discard their own mannerisms, characteristics, and psychological armor. They disavow their own *being* and become another being onstage. Although actors use their personal resources to inform their character, their own personality must disappear and dissolve inside the character they are portraying. They do this to honor the playwright, the text and their role. Actors must shed their own personae, often to the detriment of their psychological well-being. It's as if they are two people — the actor and the character.

I am what I do is the belief of many actors, as they define themselves by their art form. As they struggle with their psychological boundaries, many act out. Acting often encourages unprofessional conduct offstage as actors are easily seduced by, and susceptible to, extending performance-suspended inhibitions and impulses into their everyday lives. Some even feel entitled to disregard psycho-social mores and live a life, as Cole Porter wrote, of "Anything Goes." Lovemaking, murderous rage, substance abuse, and madness enacted onstage can lead to alien and inappropriate behavior in ordinary life. This renders actors unsafe and unprotected in the real world when their performances are over. For them, it's not over. These actors may feel powerful and whole when performing but fragile and fragmented out in the world — struggling to regroup or find their personal identity, as Humpty Dumpty cannot be put back together again.

REFLECTION 2

How much do you define yourself by what you do professionally?

1——2——3——4——5——6——7——8

1 being the lowest and 8 being the highest.

WHAT ARE YOU SEEING?

Once actors stop using themselves as instruments of performance, they must regroup and return, if you will, to their primary characters—their own persons. How easy it is for the instrument/identity boundaries to become confused! Many actors feel as if they must choose who will survive—their instruments and the characters being portrayed or their personal identities. They are, for a time at least, lost to themselves.

> *Acting may prevent the actor from performing the role of a lifetime—himself.*

WHAT AM I: THE DANCER

A Ballerina's Nightmare: 'Am I More Than Just a Dancer?'

TILER PECK, NY TIMES, FEB. 13, 2020

Perhaps more than any other performing artists, dancers see their craft as their raison d'être. This point of view creates the question *What am I* if I'm not dancing? Does life hold significance for the dancer if not on the move?

REFLECTION 3

How much is your work a part of your being?

1——2——3——4——5——6——7——8

1 being the lowest and 8 being the highest.

WHAT ARE YOU SEEING?

It's culturally accepted that the art form frequently dominates the dancer's entire life. Yet, ironically, the average performance-life-expectancy of a classical dancer is only twenty-eight years, a few more for modern dancers. Dancers start dancing sometimes as early as two or three years old and their professional course is often chosen during latency or even earlier. Therefore, family life revolves around dance schedules, forcing many young dancers and their families to make physical and social sacrifices.

There are also psychological consequences for many dancers, as they are kept obedient, silenced, dependent, and often hungry. Dance ritual and training result in the dancers' developmental infantilization. In the world of dance, they are relegated to the status of *forever young*, as reflected in their designation of "boys and girls." Yet, the dancer has no real childhood.

The dancers' commitment to their art often results in the suspension of personal autonomy—body, mind, and spirit. *"Don't think, just move."* This line from the film "The Turning Point" highlights one of the dancer's psychological plights. Thinking for themselves is not encouraged. Discipline and compliance, obsession, and passivity are valued cultural norms. The dancer conforms, obeys, and repeats the instruction of the teacher—their master, and often, their artistic creator—which often interferes with the empowerment of discovering their own voice, leaving them uni-dimensional and unable to reach their total performance potential.

Since the dancer's body is his or her instrument, body image and body mechanics are major psychological preoccupations. Their search for perfection is never-ending. Dancers have three tenets: *"Dance through the pain," "I can never be too thin," and "My body knows no limitations."* In order to support these beliefs, dancers must not only be in denial, they must also be great rationalizers, such as, *"I've never had a period, but I'll worry about that later."* However, these beliefs often result in emotional and physical injury, and physiological abnormalities, as dancers are hesitant to ask for help or be aware of when enough is enough.

Dancers are accustomed to being objectified. Since the entire body is the dancers' instrument of performance, their bodies cause considerable worry. Many live with the ever-present fear of injury. Dancers are hyper-vigilant; one wrong step can end their dreams as well as all their hard work and sacrifice. Their nightmares are filled with missteps and anxiety. What would they do? Not only would dancers be unable to dance—which feels like death itself—but very few dance companies provide medical insurance.

In addition, the art of dance demands the change or contortion, as some believe, of the natural alignment of the body. Dancers have literally come into my office with bloodied feet as if this was the natural order of things. Many are regularly weighed and scrutinized as if they were things — instruments of the dance. *"Doesn't everybody?"* were the words of a dancer in my office as he bemoaned a weight gain of two ounces.

REFLECTION 4

How preoccupied are you with your body image?

1——2——3——4——5——6——7——8
1 being the lowest and 8 being the highest.

WHAT ARE YOU SEEING?

How much does it impact your performance potential?

1——2——3——4——5——6——7——8
1 being the lowest and 8 being the highest.

WHAT ARE YOU SEEING?

Although the language of dance is richly communicative, dance is a non-verbal art form. Dancers speak in space, motion, and touch, which often places them at an enormous psychological disadvantage in the "real world," as they may not be as fluid with verbal language as they are with their bodies. Many function best non-verbally. Some dancers suffer in their personal relationships because they don't have the basic social skills and tools. Sometimes even maintaining eye contact is difficult. Although social media has greatly enhanced the dancer's ability to communicate with the non-dancing world, many don't focus on anything but dance. They're often home-schooled, and from there taken directly into the dance world. Dance is their blood and bones.

TABLEAU THREE: FELIX

"What can I do if I can't dance?" Felix, thirty-four years-old, had been injured three times and had undergone two surgeries when he entered therapy. He was in a very prominent classical dance company and had suddenly been given notice. Felix doubted his value and purpose if he could not dance. He had been dancing since he was three and with his company since he was ten. As he sat down on my couch, Felix said, "I just have to move." And even as he spoke, Felix was in motion — hands, body, feet, face — it was actually quite a beautiful therapy. At times it looked like his tears were even dancing.

Felix's therapy revolved around understanding that he didn't have to perform to continue to function as a dancer and as an artist. But first, Felix had to mourn — to find other ways to do what he did for love. He slowly let go of the idea that the only thing he could do was dance and began to recognize that he could use the gifts that he developed as a dancer in other areas for the rest of his life. He came to accept that he could function using his abilities as a dancer in different and creative ways.

As Felix moved from my therapy couch to the stage in my office, change came when he realized that he would always dance, as a performer on the stage of life. Felix became aware that his discipline, commitment, sense of precision, acute focus, fearlessness, his wonderful ability to collaborate developed from his early years in the corps, his quirky imagination, and the passion that he brought to his art form would be invaluable in whatever he did. Felix used the creativity that he poured into dancing to become a choreographer and a set designer.

Ten months after Felix left the company he married, and two years later the couple adopted a daughter, who is currently in the corps de ballet of Felix's former company.

Where am I: The Musician

The musical arts encompass two art forms: the instrumental arts and the vocal arts. Each has its own existential question. For both instrumental and vocal artists, music is their way of thinking and feeling.

What is music?
Sounds combined in such a way as to produce beauty
of form, harmony, and expression of emotion.
An art of sound in time that expresses ideas and emotions in
significant forms through the elements of rhythm,
melody, harmony, and color.
Musical sounds are periodic and somewhat regular.
They are pleasing to our ears and minds; sound has been one of the
greatest forms of expression since the beginning of time.
Unpleasant sound is often described as noise.
Noise is more irregular.
Music is a form of communication.

Although music is also called the universal language, I have found that those who "speak" it—instrumental musicians—are faced with challenges and conflicts of relatedness, belonging, and status. Music-makers are in an art form where they are constantly asking existential questions about their place in their world: *Where am I? Where do I fit in? Where do I belong?*

REFLECTION 5

How often do you wonder Where do I fit in?

1——2——3——4——5——6——7——8
1 being the lowest and 8 being the highest.

WHAT ARE YOU SEEING?

Perhaps these questions, particularly questions of relatedness, start very early in a music-maker's life. As children, musicians frequently have a very primary and intense relationship with their music teacher. Many teachers micro-manage their students, telling them what to do, taking over parental responsibilities. For impressionable young musicians, this can make for a difficult or confusing relationship with their parents, as some don't know where they belong in the teacher/parent triangle. Parents often feel left out, abandoned even, creating anxiety and stress for the entire family. And some musicians tend to seek out these kinds of teachers in college and throughout their adult lives, as they continue to struggle with questions of *Where is my place? What is my status?*

Most musicians have spent much of their time alone and isolated at home or in a practice studio with their instrument as their primary relationship. What is the psychological influence of having a piano, oboe, cello, or snare drum—an inanimate object—as your best friend? Is it any wonder that many musicians tell me that they feel strange, lonely, even lost among other people?

More specifically, many tell me they feel socially out of tune with those outside of their profession, and describe feeling clumsy, inadequate, ignorant and conspicuously different. On subjects other than music, such as politics, medicine, or even theater, it's often very difficult for them to be articulate and engage.

REFLECTION 6

*How comfortable are you when talking about
anything other than your work?*

1——2——3——4——5——6——7——8
1 being the lowest and 8 being the highest.

WHAT ARE YOU SEEING?

Like dance, instrumental music is a non-verbal art form. However, unlike dancers, instrumental musicians perceive the world in sound, intervals, pitch, and rhythms. They tell me that when in conversation—because they're listening to sound and silences between sounds, to the timing in speech patterns and to speech intonations—their verbal, reasoning, and social skills are often compromised and awkward. Some confess to numbing themselves with mind-altering substances as a way to feel more comfortable. Many instrumental musicians don't even like to socialize with singers or dancers or actors because what musicians are interested in and passionate about is music. Consequently, when they're not studying, practicing or rehearsing, which is how many spend much of their time, they attempt to fit in by socializing with other musicians.

Why?

Because they share the universal language of music. They feel that here, at last and at least, they belong. They know what to do... they make music together and they know what to talk about. Musicians absolutely love to talk about music. They talk about Mozart, Ellington, Ella, and Elgar; they talk about minor 7^{ths}, major 5^{ths} and who played them which ways; they talk about who's recording this and who's recorded that, and whose arrangements they love; anything as long as they can talk about music. They talk eloquently, brilliantly, and imaginatively and yes, when they have nothing more to say they talk about music. Yet competition with peers is rampant, which of course creates additional seclusion and estrangement. Nigel Kennedy expressed the plight of musicians when he said that they strive to be "the first rat in the race."

Personal relationships are often based on musical acuity. A percussionist described to me, in the most vivid terms, how musicians determine friendship or even more intimate relationships. "My friends," she said, "are decided not on the basis of loyalty or fun or whether they're good people but rather on how good their musicianship is, their devotion to music, how much they practice." And I find this kind of judgment jeopardizes performance potential.

Status looms large as the question: *Where do I fit in?* plays out in the musician's artistic life. Musicians respond to this question in vertical and hierarchical ways, much like chords or triads on a musical score. *Am I a soloist? If so, am I the best? Am I an ensemble or orchestral musician? If so, do I play principal or am I a section player? Am I an orchestral or just a band player?*

String players deem themselves the aristocrats—the bluebloods—of the music world. They are socialized to think they are superior to all other instrumentalists. String players have created a musical class system based on two belief systems: one, having the most prolific repertoire, and two, the belief that most pieces of music—save a cappella works—would not exist without at least one string player, regardless of the size of their musical group. They view every other type of musician as lesser and lower.

These are value judgments that have become ritualized and almost cult-like and although they are not always expressed, or even consciously recognized by many musicians, they certainly wreak havoc with professional and personal relationships.

This hierarchical thinking can cause pianists, wind players, horn players, and percussionists to experience inner conflict: worry, guilt, anxiety, obsessive thinking, and self-loathing. They may perseverate, feel inferior, be continually self-doubting, second-guessing and outcome oriented, judgmental, easily slighted, and metaphorically homeless. As for the string players, because they are the kings and queens of the kingdom, these challenges and conflicts are magnified.

Questions of status also play out as some musicians maintain that every instrument has its own personality or character. I've been told that trumpeters are selfish while flute players are more generous. Fee structures confer status. Most principal oboists in orchestras are paid more than other principals. Jazz and ensembles playing the same halls command different nightly payments. Rock groups, rappers, old timers, country artists of renown are all paid different amounts in the same performance halls. All these rankings can be destabilizing.

REFLECTION 7

How much do you believe that you fit in?

1——2——3——4——5——6——7——8
1 being the lowest and 8 being the highest.

WHAT ARE YOU SEEING?

How much does belonging impact your performance potential?

1——2——3——4——5——6——7——8
1 being the lowest and 8 being the highest.

WHAT ARE YOU SEEING?

Although music may be, for many of us, intensely moving, uplifting and a profound comfort, music-making can be isolating and alienating for the music-makers.

Why am I: The Vocal Artist

I believe that the vocal arts pose a significant challenge to the realization of an artist's performance potential. Inherent in the art form of the vocal artist is the most difficult of human explorations — existence. The question of existence deeply molds the artist's personality.

Singers are the only musicians who perform on instruments that are housed within their bodies. They are human carrying cases for instruments that they cannot see, touch, or hear. Sound is the only testament to the existence of the human voice. Vocal sound is born as air passes through the lips of the mouth much like infants are born through the lips of the genitalia. However, as with fire, which doesn't ignite by itself, sound needs something else to verify and validate its existence. Vocal artists can become totally dependent on the ears of others. These singers are often unable to realize their performance potential, as they are not able to rely on themselves to execute the techniques they have developed to create the sound they desire.

In addition, singers often refer to their instruments as *The Voice*. They speak of *The Voice* as if it were a tangible object, as if it exists outside the human skeleton. Many want to have a "life" apart from their invisible instrument. They long to put their instrument on the shelf and go out dancing. Yet *The Voice* can't be left at home. Thus, some singers overcompensate by making themselves ultra-visible. It's as if they're saying, *When you see me, you see my voice.* Some singers are notorious for attention-seeking fashion while others become the brunt of jokes, particularly in the opera world: "It's not over till the fat lady sings." The flamboyant singer often lives with stressful financial debt while the obese singer lives with health problems and professional limitations. Both can be subject to ridicule.

The invisibility of the singer's instrument has other consequences. Because vocal artists have no choice as to the material or architecture of their instruments, singers are often referred to as "non-musicians." Some singers dismiss this characterization but others take it personally, feeling insulted and diminished.

Moreover, the fragility of the human voice makes it extremely vulnerable to dietary modifications, biochemical shifts, and mood swings, as well as environmental change, including travel. Airplanes, literal germ factories, are many singers' home away from home. Many singers land at their destinations sick. Everything and anything affects the singers' instrument. A singer's health concerns run the gamut from understandable worry to preoccupation to paralyzing obsession. Singers can become over-reliant on their physicians. The self-care they require is extraordinary. If it rains, if they have steak or milk products, if somebody sneezes at a party, whether a room is too dry or too moist, whether there's pollen in the air are real concerns for them. A vocal artist's very body can feel traitorous. Menstruation affects a singer's chords, as can the slightest dehydration. Singers must also be hypersensitive to age, as it determines vocal register and repertoire: too young and too heavy, *The Voice* is ruined; too old and too high, *The Voice* is lost. Singers themselves often feel as vulnerable as their precarious instruments.

Most singers have developed beautifully honed vocal techniques that allow them to sing and perform above many bronchial illnesses. They work hard to stay well and healthy and spend a great amount of time on vocal rest. However, health-related cancellations do happen. Singers are frightened of injuring their instruments—they do not want nodes to develop; they do not want to injure their chords. Although many singers are not hypochondriacal or whimsical cancellers, many will be accused of diva-like behavior and earn bad reputations. It's a catch-22. Illness, cancellation, and efforts to stay healthy all affect a singer's performance potential. Feelings of helplessness due to the vast number of factors beyond their control cannot be overestimated.

When singers stop singing, there is a negative effect on the brain. When not singing, the amount of dopamine produced is drastically diminished and the brain networks that are activated are reduced. When singers can't sing, it alters their brain functions and they may become severely depressed.

According to Professor Sarah Wilson from The University of Melbourne, Australia, singing is a form of natural therapy in two ways: 1) singing is a positive mood-altering art form, releasing dopamine, the social bonding hormone, and 2) singing activates wonderful brain networks: motor, auditory, planning and organization, memory, language, and emotional, stimulating a surge of positive emotional feelings, such as empathy. Even thinking about singing lifts the mood and stimulates the brain.

REFLECTION 8

How much does singing affect your mood?

1——2——3——4——5——6——7——8
1 being the lowest and 8 being the highest.

WHAT ARE YOU SEEING?

*"I never know if The Voice is going to be there
when I open my mouth to sing."*

Many singers believe "I am my voice." Therefore, when *The Voice* is not met with approval, when *The Voice* is not reviewed in high estimation, when *The Voice* is not chosen in audition, when *The Voice* cannot produce, many vocal artists question *Why am I?* When singers identify with their voice, they question their own existence. When their self-esteem is founded on the quality of their sound, they question their reason to be. Some spiral into deep grief, others stop performing altogether. Some take the question of existence into their own hands.

Sometimes The Voice seems like The Enemy.

REFLECTION 9

How much do you question your reason to be?

1——2——3——4——5——6——7——8
1 being the lowest and 8 being the highest.

WHAT ARE YOU SEEING?

How much does it impact your performance potential?

1——2——3——4——5——6——7——8

1 being the lowest and 8 being the highest.

WHAT ARE YOU SEEING?

Who am I? What am I? Where am I? Why am I?

How the individual artist chooses to cope with the psychological perils unique to each art form will impact and influence their performance potential.

THE MISSION OF THE PERFORMING ARTIST

The performing artists of the earliest culture had a mission that was both survivalistic and ritualistic in nature. Their primary mission was to honor and revere their audience of gods and nature. Today, notwithstanding their differences, actors, dances, musicians and vocal artists are united by their culture's mission. Performing Artists are passionate about creating a transformative experience for their audiences. Whether it's an audience of one or thousands, experienced live or from the comfort of home, performers want to move their audiences, subtly changing them, inside and out. They do this through storytelling.

What a privilege and what a burden!

Artists allow us to understand ourselves, helping us to experience our emotions. Experiencing an actor tell the story of Willy Loman in *Death of a Salesman,* Joaquin Phoenix as the Joker, Tatiana Osipova dancing Giselle, or Christine Goerke as Brunhilde, helps audiences confront the stories of their own broken hopes and dreams.

They not only reflect our most dire moments but also our most celebratory ones. Taylor Swift shaking it off, Pharrell saluting life with "Happy," and the joy in Beethoven's "Fidelio," when Leonora, frees her husband from imminent death, is palpable. All give testimony that we are not alone.

"I cry every time I hear that song"

How often has a singer, dancer, actor or musician taken us to a dark place that we've avoided or couldn't quite reach? Performing artists enable us to tune into a primal part of ourselves. Bernadette Peters singing Sondheim, Pinkerton's cry "Butterfly, Butterfly," the sounds of Janis Joplin, Audra McDonald in "Lady Day," or the twelve double basses sounding the opening chord of Wagner's Ring Cycle—seem to explain so many things we might otherwise struggle to come to grips with.

"They get me"

Because many performers can cause us to feel such a profound sense of being understood and touched, a feeling of oneness, of unity, a symbiosis may develop. It's as if we've become a part of the creative process… as if we've evoked

Pinkerton's response, Lady Day's collapse, or Janis Joplin's pathos. This transcendence appears to make the connection almost physical.

REFLECTION 10

How open are you to allowing an artist to touch your heart and transform you?

1——2——3——4——5——6——7——8
1 being the lowest and 8 being the highest.

WHAT ARE YOU SEEING?

What piece of music, aria, dance or drama touches your heart and can bring you to tears?

WHAT ARE YOU SEEING?

Through their ability to tell a story, artists connect us to the past, present, and future. Across the centuries, performers have used history's darkest moments to inform. Gary Oldman as Winston Churchill in "Darkest Hour" and Liam Neeson as Oskar Schindler in "Schindler's List" masterfully portrayed these important men allowing their audiences to experience the weight of World War II. The brilliant performers in the musical drama "Hamilton" reflect history as it is rarely depicted, and in doing so enlighten and educate their public.

Performing artists also help to expand our connection to the world at large as different places, cultures, and environments are explored. In Disney's "Fantasia," the stories are performed by musicians who bring to life the classical scores of Tchaikovsky, Schubert, Beethoven, Mussorgsky, and of course Prokofiev's "Sorcerer's Apprentice." The performer's voices behind the film's animated characters communicate the polemic of good vs. evil, the evolution of the planet, and the extinction of the dinosaurs. We need only to look at global warming and ask, has the past taught us anything?

When we listen to great jazz artists, we can hear them "speaking" among themselves. They encourage collaboration, conversation and communication. They demonstrate the art of engagement and relationship through improvisation and musical arrangements. Jazz and chamber musicians and especially members of the *corps de ballet* talk to me about trust. They are experts in "active" listening. Trust is the foundation of artistic relationships and is so essential to the integrity of each art form. However, I have found that trust between artists comes only after they trust themselves.

REFLECTION 11

How much do you trust yourself?

1——2——3——4——5——6——7——8
1 being the lowest and 8 being the highest.

WHAT ARE YOU SEEING?

As a way to support their mission, performing artists are superlative empathizers of the human condition. They articulate and raise social consciousness. They've taught me that they use both their art form and their empathy to give their audiences a way to gain a deeper understanding of their friends, families, colleagues, communities, and themselves. The dancers of the Alvin Ailey American Dance Theater, in Robert Battle's "The Hunt," brings into awareness contemporary social issues through their passion and individual expressiveness. In the 1930's, Martha Graham, one of the first modern dancers and choreographers, used dramatic movement to provide insight into and identification with the female psyche. Current artists such as Chance the Rapper with his album "Coloring Book" and Childish Gambino with "This is America" allow audiences to walk in the shoes of another.

Artists in the time of Covid, when their inspiration is most needed, were silenced. Their performance venues were darkened. Their worth dismissed and their absence hardly mentioned outside of their culture with all that is going on.

However, artists will not be quieted; their art will not be suppressed!

Using technologies far too numerous for me to cite, artists all over the world perform and perform passionately, fearlessly, creatively, committed to follow their mission… *especially* in the time of Covid.

Through storytelling, performing artists use their music, dance and drama to fulfill their mission … to make a difference.

THE CULTURAL HURDLES, HARDSHIPS, AND HAZARDS PERFORMERS FACE

Like every culture, performing artists face their share of occupational hurdles, professional hardships and psychological hazards. How they handle these hurdles, hardships and hazards determines their personality profile and influences their performance potential.

Occupational Hurdles

The world of entertainment is not always entertaining for the entertainers. The storytellers tell me stories of occupational hurdles that are deeply rooted in their culture. Performing artists live a *lifestyle* where the only certainty is uncertainty. Inherent in their culture are four uncertainties:

- financial insecurity
- geographic relocations
- a topsy-turvy sense of time, and
- relationship instability…

and they're all interrelated

REFLECTION 12

Circle the cultural built-ins that impact your lifestyle

Financial Insecurity

Geographic Relocations

Topsy-turvy Sense of Time

Relationship Instability

WHAT ARE YOU SEEING?

FINANCIAL INSECURITY

Financial insecurity in the performing arts is a harsh cultural norm—toxic to all other aspects of an artist's life. Artists expect that there will be employment peaks and valleys, as very few performers work all the time. It is the nature of the culture. However, the depth and breadth of the peaks and valleys can be devastating, and many artists of remarkable potential have made the painful decision to leave the profession because they needed to survive.

A *working* performer is an artist making a living wage over time. For artists to stay viable, they must practice, train, audition, and network regularly, and this takes time, energy, and *money*. Most artists must expect to do temporary work at some point in their artistic careers, and this can impact their ability to *practice, train, audition, and network*, which in turn can interfere with their performance potential.

TABLEAU FOUR: AMY

Amy, in her twenties and living in the city, came to see me because she was having financial issues. She was a jazz singer who was going through the usual feast and famine. She came from a wealthy family in a neighboring state and her father wanted her to return home and join his very lucrative catering business where she could have made a very comfortable living. Amy felt very conflicted. She was feeling a tug to return home but her calling was music. During the course of the therapy, she determined that she needed to be true to herself and generate another form of income in addition to her musical life. She decided to develop a networking business for artists. She was very personable, very capable and competent. If people needed housing or needed to know about school districts or tutoring, she would do the research and connect them. She became extremely successful in her temporary business and actually really enjoyed it. Amy knew a lot of people in the artistic community who needed basic information. As a creative, Amy used her creativity in a way that supported her financially. Her conflict was resolved, her anxiety about supporting herself disappeared. Amy didn't move back home, and went on to have a good jazz career. But...she still kept the family entrepreneurial spirit alive!

Some artists will take work just for the money, which also affects their performance potential because they "phone it in" and devalue themselves and the art form. In addition, most artists have to reimagine their standard of living not only between gigs but even when they're working steadily. Fame and fortune is relative for every performer. Many must lower their expectations of what this means, as often only well-known artists can command decent fees.

Although uncertainty accompanies life upon the wicked stage, I have learned that financial insecurity is the most insidious. How true is this for everyone who works?

True financial success for performing artists can also be compared to a lottery: *one in a million*. Frequently, regardless of talent or hours spent training, practicing, and auditioning, an artist's success comes down to timing and luck. Being in the right place at the right time. Who saw you, who heard you? Who do you know?

REFLECTION 13

How true is this in your work?

1———2———3———4———5———6———7———8
1 being the lowest and 8 being the highest.

WHAT ARE YOU SEEING?

Networking (v.): the action or process of interacting with others to exchange information and develop professional or social contacts—also feeds financial well-being.

How many times have each of us heard that? Networking as well as politicking plays such a huge role that talent and the artist's history are often not enough. What is your network and how *well* do you network? Much of networking is so intentional and intelligent. In show business, it is often said that one must *network or not work*. Building relationships with others is almost as important as doing the work itself. Decision- makers are willing to look at a performer who is recommended by someone they know and respect. We've all heard the saying, "In Hollywood, it's not what you know, it's *who* you know."

However, many performers develop creative occupational obstacle-solving. When faced with financial insecurity, performers can learn how to manage or create money in inventive ways.

REFLECTION 14

How much does financial insecurity affect your performance potential?

1——2——3——4——5——6——7——8

1 being the lowest and 8 being the highest.

WHAT ARE YOU SEEING?

GEOGRAPHIC RELOCATIONS

How do performers create a home base if they don't know how long they'll be living there?

"I don't know where I'm going to work."

"I don't know where I'm going to live."

"I don't know if I'm going out on tour, or for how long." "

Should I purchase?"

"Should I rent?" "Should I sublet?"

"I don't want to live with other people."

"I want to live alone."

"Does my contract pay for housing?"

While touring may appear glamorous on the outside, most often it's anything but alluring and fun. Geographic relocations are often filled with unpredictability and conflict. It's a cultural probability- working performers tour constantly. The different places and climates that performers tour affect wardrobe, laundry, diet, and cooking; the type and amount of alcohol and other substances consumed; sleeping and circadian rhythms. Touring impacts money: telephone bills, socializing, TV watching, and social media habits.

Life on the road separates performers from friends and family, which creates intense loneliness. A Zoom a day does not maintain attachments. These changes can destabilize anyone and everyone. When the tour is over, artists must re-enter their home base. This can be challenging. Both coming and going can negatively impact performance potential.

Still, some learn to love being lifelong travelers. When on tour, they can discover the country, see a lot of the world they might not have otherwise seen. They're exposed to different cultures, they hear different languages, experience different foods and lifestyles. If they're careful, many can save money. If artists are adventuresome, they can use these experiences to inform their art and their life, and how they show up, onstage and off, to reach their performance potential.

REFLECTION 15

How much do geographic relocations affect
your performance potential?

1——2——3——4——5——6——7——8
1 being the lowest and 8 being the highest.

WHAT ARE YOU SEEING?

TOPSY-TURVY SENSE OF TIME

When performers are working, their days and nights are upside down. Their productivity, purpose and energy peak at night because live performances are primarily in the evening. Instead of working 9 AM to 5 PM most performing artists work from 5 PM to 9 AM. While artists are performing, most of the world—including their loved ones—is winding down or asleep. This affects their entire lifestyle: relationships, health, and day-to-day activities.

Post-show, it's difficult for artists to unwind and get to sleep when adrenaline and cortisol are coursing through their veins and circadian rhythms don't know which beat to follow. The artist's energy goes up and it has to come down.

It's difficult for many performers to schedule anything with those who work on the other side of the clock. Rachel Brosnahan, the star of the Netflix mega-hit The Marvelous Mrs. Maisel, was reported saying: "These days, I find it difficult to have any kind of set routine because my schedule seems to be constantly in flux."

Many performing artists often don't know when or if they're going to work, which certainly adds to the uncertainty of their lifestyle. They wait and wait and wait. It's very disruptive to them and those around them. Many wait by their phone—or, more accurately, as I see in my office every day—they check their phones constantly.

When not actively performing, it's very difficult for artists to readjust their internal clocks and return to an "ordinary" 9 to 5 life. Many take day jobs—which can interfere with auditioning and their psychological well-being, while others experience unstructured time with nothing to keep them busy. Both impede their performance potential.

Nevertheless, some adjust to their topsy-turvy schedules, finding ways to use time imaginatively and shape a healthy work/life balance when not performing. Motivation, discipline and creativity are called for. It is important for them to create a strict schedule with very specific activities, including exercise. I've found that it takes artists at least two weeks to change their circadian rhythms and get back to a non-performing lifestyle.

REFLECTION 16

How much does your work schedule affect your performance potential?

1——2——3——4——5——6——7——8
1 being the lowest and 8 being the highest.

WHAT ARE YOU SEEING?

Relationship Instability

Personal relationships in this business are very precarious and often play second fiddle. Every artist from each of the art forms is susceptible to relationship challenges which put into jeopardy their performance potential and impact their personality development.

Whether on the road or at home, whether an artist is attached or unattached, when actors join a new cast, when orchestras or dancers go into a new season, when vocal artists go on tour they form new and powerful connections. They spend their time with other artists, and whether it's for a night or three months or three years, they become artificially-related families. They share a special language– a language they don't share with their partners and children at home.

When actors bond in a cast they actually become two families: the family of the story line and the family of actors. They're double-bonded. And at the end of the run, separation can be difficult. "Falling in love" within a given production is common. Returning to their real families, with laundry, banking, grocery shopping, school—'mundane living'—often pales in comparison.

And when dancers perform, the exhilaration is so hypnotic that it's hard to even speak about it—and the joy and ecstasy it evokes—to a non-dancing human. Dancing is a very physical art. Dancers touch each other all the time and they know each other's bodies so completely. The familiarity of this kind of connection often leads to sexual intimacy.

When musicians are surrounded by music of their own making, it's hard to imagine the seductive power that music has on them. It unites them with one another, bonding them in a way that can exclude all other relationships.

REFLECTION 17

How closely bonded are you to your fellow artists or colleagues?

1——2——3——4——5——6——7——8
1 being the lowest and 8 being the highest.

WHAT ARE YOU SEEING?

Even when not in performance, singers gravitate to one another. Whether operatic, jazz, pop, or blues, vocal artists have a special connection because they understand what it means to carry an invisible instrument. When on vocal rest—isolating them in silence from others—singers are further bonded with their own community of singers. When in performance, such as in an opera, the spectacle, the majesty, and the power of the music are so overwhelming that intimate relationships often develop. In addition, the singer/conductor relationship is often intense, the communication between them so powerful that it often leads to liaisons. All these factors create instability in established relationships and may estrange the singer from loved ones.

When performing artists talk to me about going on the road and into sheltered halls where they spend their time, they explain to me how they become powerfully connected with their orchestras, cast members, repertoire companies, and their performing arts communities. This is particularly intense because a working performer may not meet many people outside of his immediate cast, ensemble, or orchestra.

Intimacy and commitment, on and offstage, can be an issue for performing artists. How many of us kiss or die, follow a stick, or stand on our toes to make a living? All of which create such passion, such bonding, and demand such commitment that there's hardly time for performers to engage in anything but the art form or with anyone other than fellow artists in pursuit of the same endeavor. The fervor for their art can never be underestimated. The intensity, and the otherworldliness of it takes the performing artist out of the reality of their daily lives. It's the sound created by their music making, the ardent delivery of their text, or the heat generated between them that disrupts relationships in their personal lives. When performers are in an embrace onstage, they can easily get carried away in the moment. *Showmances* are the rule, not the exception.

SHOWMANCES

TABLEAU FIVE:
LOUISE AND HENRY

When Louise and Henry sang "There's a Place for Us" from Bernstein's "West Side Story," the audience believed them. Why shouldn't they? They'd been hooking up for the previous nine weeks. Their showmance began ten days into rehearsal. Each was married to someone else; each had a family. Henry had a year-old child. At the end of the run, Louise came into therapy heartbroken and unable to be intimate with her husband.

TABLEAU SIX: MARYLOU

Marylou came back into therapy after a six-year absence as devastated as I'd ever seen her.

"I had an affair," she said. "And I don't know what to do. I'm still in contact with him. It was so romantic; the lines we delivered just came alive through the magic of what we were feeling. I'm thinking of leaving my husband, whom I still adore."

TABLEAU SEVEN: ANTONIO

"I can't help it if they think I'm God. And now my wife wants to leave me. I fall deeply in love with someone from each new production and she becomes my inspiration. Can I help it if she loves me back? I love my wife, she's like my right arm, I love my children, but I have to have a muse; I have to. I feel like I'm dead without another muse. And my wife just does not understand! I'm an artist! Can you help me?"

TABLEAU EIGHT: CYRUS AND JEFFREY

Dancers Cyrus and Jeffrey met on tour and fell head over heels in love. Cyrus had just ended a five-year relationship. The tour, which was to take them to four continents, was to last fifteen months. Jeffrey felt pretty secure in the longevity of the relationship. Sixteen months later he was in my office. His heart was broken. He was telling me he felt like a convenience to Cyrus, as though the tour was a cocoon in an unreal world, where he couldn't see reality. He felt like a prop.

REFLECTION 18

How much does relationship instability affect your performance potential?

1——2——3——4——5——6——7——8

1 being the lowest and 8 being the highest.

WHAT ARE YOU SEEING?

In spite of the new and powerful connections, many performing artists resist the special bonding and gain an increased awareness of how special their existing personal relationships are.

Professional Hardships

The culture of the performing artist hosts a duo of interconnected, professional hardships. It is unstable and self-serving. Recognition and wealth, epitomizing these hardships, are normative cultural built-ins. However, artists tell me stories in which pursuing and achieving fame and fortune come at great personal cost, affecting their personalities as well as their performance potential.

INSTABILITY

All actors, dancers, musicians and vocal artists—regardless of their level of success—are subject to the opinions, agendas, and whims of all the other players and institutions in their culture. There are many people pulling strings and exerting their needs and desires. While instability is intrinsic within the profession, public judgment—from fans and nonfans—can cause performers to feel particularly unstable.

Performers can become self-conscious, or, as I refer to it, *other*-conscious—when they stop being themselves and become performers who *impress* rather than *express*. When focused on crowd-pleasing, performers are unable to concentrate on their music, dance, script or song, and ultimately lose their personal voice. As a consequence, their self-esteem is diminished. These performers compromise themselves.

A devastated bass player wept as he said, " I tried to fulfill their expectations at the cost of my artistry and devalued my performance potential."

List three situations in your work life when you impress.

List three situations in your work life when you express.

Very often, the expectations of the public are totally unrealistic and capricious. And the ease with which everyone is able to generate and share content across the various social media platforms has exacerbated the effects of these expectations. Privacy seems to be a thing of the past. No one is exempt.

While social media has many benefits—producers, networks, marketers, and of course performers, are able to reach their public quickly and directly—it also has its drawbacks and obstacles. Many artists manage their own social media accounts. Their need to share content and showcase a certain lifestyle, often with the desire to increase exposure and delight and grow their fan base, can backfire. The public responds to tweets and posts immediately and vociferously, which means the performer is constantly being judged and fed expectations. They are no longer solely reliant on the critics—professionals who critique the merits of artistic or musical works—for their primary source of feedback. Some even believe that critics are becoming almost obsolete. What performers are left with is uncensored, emotional responses to anything and everything performers reveal, or don't. This lack of filter can be refreshing but it can also be devastating and destabilizing. Performers tell me they often feel like prey.

REFLECTION 19

How much does social media figure in your life?

1——2——3——4——5——6——7——8
1 being the lowest and 8 being the highest.

WHAT ARE YOU SEEING?

Today, as mobile devices are pervasive and information is transmitted instantaneously, the public can make or break a performer and a performance. Everything—every kiss, every bad hair day, every sound bite, every pound, every image, provocative or not—is captured and shared on a constant basis. The concept of word of mouth takes on new meaning.

More and more performing artists are contributing to their own rise and fall. They read about how they're loved and adored and hated and despised. This barometer of love/hate affects them daily and impacts their performance potential.

REFLECTION 20

How important is the approval of others in your work?

1——2——3——4——5——6——7——8
1 being the lowest and 8 being the highest.

WHAT ARE YOU SEEING?

Although the public appears to admire their favorite performers, it is thrilled by their falls from grace. Performers are idealized then devalued. Public voyeurism provides a diva-addicted culture with a delusional escape into scandal from ordinary life. The public revels in any tidbit of gossip. Public envy destroys performers for what they seem to possess—sex, money, and power. How can any performer trust the praise and the adoration without becoming anxious or even a little paranoid? And the absence of truth, privacy, and loyalty can be personally and professionally destabilizing.

The public often acts as if it *owns* its performing artists. And indeed, performers talk to me about feeling owned or possessed. Boundaries, especially given the ubiquity of social media, are tenuous at best. The public feels that they possess their artists and the artists owe them something in return for their interest. *"I feel like I'm owned, and this really throws me off-balance,"* a noted film actor confessed. The sense of being possessed is in itself demoralizing, as life feels out of their control—artists often don't experience their own sense of agency.

Many performing artists train—often at great sacrifice—to become the best they can be. The public supports and praises them for their special gifts and talents. And then they falter: They hit a bad note, there's a wardrobe malfunction, or they look fat in a bikini. Those who cheered and praised these artists, who looked up to them and adored them, suddenly turn on them, seemingly taking a perverse pleasure in their failing and falling. I have seen the devastating effect that their fickleness can have on the artist's performance potential both onstage and off.

The current #MeToo Movement has resulted in many artists falling from grace. The entertainment industry made an example of the predators and the public was quick to weigh in, despising those they once idolized. Idealized and devalued. Alone and devastated, these performing artists are left to heal their wounds and wonder what might have been.

TABLEAU NINE: SADIE

Sadie had been in film and television for over thirty-five years when she came to me at fifty-seven. She had come out a week before in the #MeToo movement. Although her fans embraced her participation in the movement, in her own eyes, Sadie had fallen from grace. As she sat on my couch she was visibly shaking, and she shook through the first several sessions that we met. At one point she vomited in my waste basket. Her public persona and her therapy persona couldn't have been more different. "I have no regret publicly revealing my sexual experiences, but I really feel responsible for what happened," she told me. Although she was publicly vehement and assertive about the abusive and degrading behavior of several directors with whom she had worked for many years, what we talked about in the office was her shame, guilt and self-loathing. It wasn't until the last five or ten years that women began to become empowered and to question industry mores. It took some time before Sadie began to understand that it was the self-serving nature of the industry that allowed such behavior and how expected and accepted it was. Sadie and I continue to work together and she is slowly rebuilding her self-esteem and starting to forgive herself.

I've also worked with some male performers who came to me full of regret because of their inappropriate sexual behaviors. They were surprised because, in some way, it almost felt like they had an agreement with the devil—in the past, the culture presumed a kind of Faustian arrangement that inflamed their fantasies of being special and immune to the outcome of their sexual whims and actions. When they were called out, these performers were forced to abandon the idea that they were God's gift to performing. Impotence supplanted their false sense of importance. Alienation and panic replaced their entitlement. And these deflated artists felt left alone with their rage, regret, and acute mortification. Through our work, they are now understanding that their glaringly conspicuous attitudes of inflated worth and bad behavior have consequences which will result in their fall from grace. Many are beginning to show remorse.

The unpredictable nature of the profession can cause further disequilibrium among the most hard-working performers. Competition—which is a valued cultural norm—plays a big roll. In part, competition is an outgrowth of scarcity, as the demand for work is so much greater than the supply of available jobs. Even great performers are sacrificed and their performance potential unsupported. And yet, rather than recognizing that the business is unstable, many blame themselves. I believe competition could have a stabilizing effect. I talk to performers about making competition positive by focusing on their personal best. However, many shift from personal best to *being better* than others.

REFLECTION 21

When you compete, how much do you focus
on being better than others?

1——2——3——4——5——6——7——8
1 being the lowest and 8 being the highest.

WHAT ARE YOU SEEING?

When you compete, how much do you focus on your personal best?

1——2——3——4——5——6——7——8
1 being the lowest and 8 being the highest.

WHAT ARE YOU SEEING?

Self-Serving

Performers do *Rush In Where Angels Fear to Tread*. This just about sums up the business of show as the culture supports the self-serving nature of the profession in several ways.

"You're only as good as your last performance" is a sentiment I hear all the time. And performing artists are often admired less for their artistry than for how much money they bring in at the box office. In fact, show business often validates the moneymakers regardless of bad behavior. It took eight seasons to kill off "Two and a Half Men"'s Charlie Harper, portrayed by Charlie Sheen, and purportedly loosely based on the actor's life. It's been reported that Sheen's very public tantrums, womanizing, drug and alcohol abuse were overlooked because his celebrity made the studio money. His bad behavior was almost titillating, until it got to be too much. His public was quick to forgive his excesses.

As Bob Sugar in the film "Jerry Maguire" says: "It's not show friends, it's show business."

From liquor to lying to sex scandals to inflated egos, the profession tolerates self-indulgent performers who show special promise. That is, until they fall from grace. In the opera world, many singers manifest diva-esque behaviors. They throw hissy fits, arrive late to rehearsals, or cancel performances. Some don't know their lines, forcing the prompter to yell so loudly that people in the front rows can hear them. But because these singers are so beloved, they get away with it… for a while. In addition, some conductors are abusive to their orchestral musicians but as long as they bring in the crowds they're allowed to carry on.

Supporting the self-serving nature of the profession are two well-known show biz myths: *The Myth of A Star is Born* and *The Myth of the Suffering Artist*. These two myths enrich the cultural lore.

The Myth of A Star is Born is pleasurable to contemplate. The idea that a performer can be discovered at any time and immediately attain fame and fortune is the stuff of which dreams are made; it's *La La land*. However, it often keeps performers active in the business in unproductive ways, as in, putting life "on hold" while *waiting* to be discovered. These performers become infertile in many ways—waiting to pursue another profession, get married, or even have children, as they procrastinate and strive for perfection. These artists are perpetually stuck with their performance potential on hold. They are in denial.

Denial (n.): the refusal or emotional inability to accept reality or fact; acting as if a painful event, thought, or feeling did not exist.

Other ways that denial is manifested and supports *The Myth of A Star is Born*:

- Some performers stay in New York when they have great geographical opportunities elsewhere, to wait for their Broadway chance.

- Some performers do too much—auditioning non-stop and never getting the gig or auditioning until the auditions are not offered any more. They do not get the message.

- When small performance opportunities do occur, the anxiety of many performers is so high that they become too competitive, too aggressive, or too timid. They don't show up well and they're not rehired.

In this myth, Lady Luck plays a big part, reinforcing their denial. Very few performers are like Sutton Foster, the Tony-award winning musical theater actor, who went from ensemble to lead in "Thoroughly Modern Millie" when the original Millie became unable to perform two weeks before opening night.

REFLECTION 22

How big a role does WAITING play in your work repertoire?

1——2——3——4——5——6——7——8
1 being the lowest and 8 being the highest.

WHAT ARE YOU SEEING?

The second myth, *The Myth of the Suffering Artist*, conditions performers to live with discontent as their lot. This myth teaches that despair, poverty, rejection, and irrationality are the natural order for artists. The myth is a romantic notion. Some use it to deny and rationalize disappointment. Others use the myth to sabotage success. Some will go into an audition unprepared. Others will come to work hung-over. Some will intentionally get into arguments with their colleagues. Anything to continue suffering as a way to fulfill the myth.

To dispel the myth, artists might ask, *"What can I do to improve?"* or *What did I learn?"* to move past the pain when, for example, they don't win an audition. They might see the suffering as a learning experience rather than as their lot in life. Unfortunately, many artists are too comfortable in the suffering and in the *"It's supposed to be like this."* Those who don't question the pain tend to wallow in it and wear it as a badge of honor.

"I am an artist. I must suffer in order to create."

Many artists come into my office and ask, "If you take away my craziness or my suffering, will I still have my genius and creativity?"

There was a time when I answered, *"Absolutely not!"*

I must suffer in order to create is a belief system for many, many performers. They truly believe that if they let go of their suffering, their talent, genius or creativity will be lost.

However, I've learned that giving them reassurance provides very little comfort. Now when they ask, I respond by saying, *"I know this is a concern and we can address it during our work."*

As with any other therapeutic concern, they can let their suffering empower them and use it to inform their art in many ways. In order to do so, they have to understand the meaning of their suffering. Rather than allowing it to control and define them, they must learn how to control and define it.

Suffering need not be a cultural norm.

Both myths prevent performing artists from reaching their performance potential.

REFLECTION 23

How much do you buy into The Myth of the Suffering Artist?

1——2——3——4——5——6——7——8
1 being the lowest and 8 being the highest.

WHAT ARE YOU SEEING?

Yet, many performers choose to be in this profession fraught with professional hardships, maintaining: *This is who I am, I have no choice.*

REFLECTION 24

How much do you believe that you have no choice?

1——2——3——4——5——6——7——8
1 being the lowest and 8 being the highest.

WHAT ARE YOU SEEING?

Psychological Hazards

They Always Knew

REFLECTION 25

At age seven, what did you want to do when you grew up?

How passionate were you?

1——2——3——4——5——6——7——8
1 being the lowest and 8 being the highest.

WHAT ARE YOU SEEING?

Did you end up doing it?

WHAT ARE YOU SEEING?

What percentage of people in this world know, when they're not yet seven or eight years old, what they want to do when they're adults?

Although everyone performs, unlike young dancers who pirouette, musicians who bow, singers who vocalize, or actors who improvise, do future dentists, plumbers or lawyers begin to drill, plunge or cross-examine when they are just children?

A huge percentage of actors, dancers, musicians, and vocal artists knew what they wanted to do and who they wanted to be at a very early age, and end up doing it. Performing has always been central to their lives.

Yannick Nézét-Séguin ☆Daniel Radcliff ☆Barbra Streisand ☆Mark Wahlberg ☆ Dame Judith Dench☆ Wynton Marsalis ☆ Maria Callas ☆ Cherry Jones ☆Frank Sinatra☆ Lady Gaga☆ Matthew Broderick ☆Mickey Rooney ☆ Dolly Parton ☆ Leonard Bernstein ☆ Lindsay Lohan ☆ Bette Davis ☆ Macaulay Culkin ☆ Drew Barrymore ☆ Cher ☆Jason Bateman ☆Wendy Whelan☆ Dakota Fanning ☆ Judy Garland ☆ Misty Copeland ☆ Brooke Shields ☆ Leonardo diCaprio ☆ Selena Gomez ☆ Justin Timberlake ☆ Shirley Temple ☆Andrew Garfield ☆ John Travolta ☆ Caruso ☆ Elizabeth Moss ☆Paul Simon ☆Henry Winkler ☆Bob Dylan ☆Beverly Sills ☆Wolfgang Amadeus Mozart ☆ Britney Spears ☆ Tim Matheson ☆ Jennifer Lopez ☆ Ludwig van Beethoven ☆ Miley Cyrus ☆ Jerry Maren ☆ Kelly Clarkson ☆Amanda Bynes ☆Ray Charles ☆ Christina Ricci ☆ Elijah Wood ☆ Anna Paquin ☆ Haley Joel Osment ☆ Emily Osment ☆ Christian Bale☆ Jacob Tremblay☆ Natalie Portman ☆ Shia LaBeouf ☆ Claire Danes ☆Twyla Tharp ☆ Lorde ☆ Michael Jackson ☆ Salma Hayek ☆ Victoria Justice ☆ Demi Lovato☆ Hilary Duff ☆ Judy Garland ☆ Maddie Ziegler ☆ Rudolf Nureyev ☆ Winona Ryder ☆ Emilio Estevez ☆ Julie Andrews ☆David Hallberg ☆Dame Maggie Smith ☆ Joni Mitchell ☆ Bradley Cooper ☆ Kurt Elling ☆ Lawrence Olivier ☆Austin Pendleton ☆ Amy Schumer ☆Anthony Michael Hall ☆ Nicole Kidman ☆Gelsey Kirkland ☆ Judd Nelson ☆Christina Aguilera ☆ Frederic Chopin ☆ Matt Damon ☆ Ally Sheedy ☆James Dean ☆Kirsten Dunst ☆Sarah Chang ☆Ralph Macchio ☆ Sarah Jessica Parker ☆ Phoebe Cates☆ River Phoenix ☆Raven Symone ☆Fred Astaire ☆ Shannen Doherty ☆Beatrice Miller ☆ Molly Ringwald ☆Louis Armstrong ☆Josh Groban ☆ Billy Joel ☆ Taylor Swift ☆ Gary Coleman ☆ Lisa Bonet ☆ Johnny Depp ☆ Millie Bobby Brown ☆Jackie Coogan ☆ Lukas Haas ☆ Candace Cameron-Bure ☆ Dylan & Cole Sprouse ☆ Alyssa Milano ☆ Abigail Breslin ☆ Mandy Moore ☆

To cite but a few...

For performing artists, *"I always knew…"* is the rule rather than the exception. And I believe that this *knowing* can be psychologically hazardous to each artist's personality development and performance potential.

Many performers know that they want to act, dance, sing or play an instrument as early as four to eight years old, the ages when—according to Erik Erikson's psycho-social stages of development—initiative and industry are the major developmental tasks. During these periods, these oft-times prodigious children develop a passion as they devote their energy and time acquiring the skills that their music, dance, or acting requires. These budding artists demonstrate confidence and creativity as they begin to explore their art as they assert, *"This is not a choice."* These young people doggedly pursue their chosen art form, be it the stage, the piano, violin, ballet, tap, or acting in curious and imaginative ways. At such tender ages, these children often demonstrate amazing competence, commitment, and sense of direction as they give the appearance of having already found meaning and purpose in their lives.

Some of the performing artists with whom I've worked and who knew at an early age that they wanted to perform, grew up in artistic families; some simply fell into it; others experienced their parents' adulation of much esteemed artists; and many others were inspired by artists with whom they felt a connection. Something had touched their hearts and they said, *"That's what I want to do and who I want to be when I grow up."* However, many others had experienced profound loss and turned to the performing arts to fill a void.

Loss

For some performers, loss involves important people in their lives—a parent, grandparent, sibling, teacher, friend, or a beloved animal. However, for many artists in my practice, there was a different kind of loss. As young people they felt that their main caretakers didn't "get" them; they felt misunderstood. Not feeling understood represented, for them, a loss of empathy. This loss of empathy left them feeling empty, and existentially lost and lonely. This loss drove these artists to find something to connect with in profound ways. These young artists turned to music, dance, singing, or acting as a way to complete themselves. They might listen to Mozart's Requiem, to Puccini, Lizzo, Billie Eilish, Eminem, Nina Simone, Wynton Marsalis, Adele… read Shakespeare, Ibsen, or August Wilson, and immediately feel understood, touched… loved. They somehow felt full and whole. It was this loss of empathy that I kept hearing over and over again—though, I hesitate to call it a *loss* in the strict sense of the word, as it was something they had never experienced. So, it was the *finding* of empathy, on their own, when they were fortunate enough, when they were young, to discover it through their art.

When have you felt misunderstood in your life?

REFLECTION 26

How much did you fill the void with your work choice?

1———2———3———4———5———6———7———8
1 being the lowest and 8 being the highest.

WHAT ARE YOU SEEING?

Ella Fitzgerald comes to mind when I think about this loss or *finding* of empathy. Ella was reported to have been a very lonely person; her music was her everything. "Fitzgerald lived for her career—and her personal life suffered… She was insecure, got nervous before performances and cried if she got a bad review. And she was overweight for much of her life." Ella always knew…

Is this "knowing" too much too soon?

On the one hand, performers who knew what they wanted to do and who they wanted to be at an early age develop such wonderful skill sets that they are often prodigiously competent, confident, and self-possessed. As young artists they are committed to a creative way of being that they have chosen, which gives them a lifelong purpose and direction. Their performance potential can thrive in large part because they have grown up with a passion and a dream.

On the other hand, an entire life/art balance can be jeopardized. Education may be skewed, ability to interact with others thwarted, family relationships challenged, and sense of self distorted. Performers may even experience value confusion and, as a result, guilt. In addition, performers may not get what they need to develop confidence, integrity, and a solid sense of identity. All this can lead to feelings of inferiority and self-doubt. Thus, performance potential cannot be realized as the performer's psycho-social development is arrested.

By the time these artists who "always knew" reach me, they are no longer children. They are adults, but the following interrelated questions remain:

- How does their culture support the young artist's transition into adulthood?

- What is the responsibility of the culture and all its players—who don't have work without their artists?

- Does the culture give them the support they need for their psychological development?

When they are working, young artists are often home-schooled. Since they have no legal rights until the age of 18, they must trust others to look out for their best interests, usually in the form of parental representation. At 18, these artists, when working, are entitled to often outrageous sums of money and don't necessarily know how to manage it.

- How equipped are young artists to handle financial success and how does their culture protect them?

- How realistic is the expectation that, because they are or were successful young child performers, they will be adult success stories? Pressure to succeed is very intense as the child transitions to adolescence and young adulthood. As these young artists mature, some of the artistic attributes of children—vulnerability, cuteness, openness, sensitivity—may not be considered attributes in the business of show in adulthood.

- How does the culture prepare young professionals, *who always knew*, when their bodies and their very beings change and evolve as they grow into adults, betraying their *always knowing*?

PERFORMING

Ironically, performing itself—acting, dancing, music-making, and singing—can be psychologically hazardous to performing artists. It can negatively affect both a performer's personality and performance potential.

In the culture of the performing artist, performing is the fulcrum around which the performer's entire life is organized. Yet, as contradictory as it may seem, performing itself can prevent artists from reaching their performance potential.

And although I will be describing performing and three of its resulting psychological hazards through the eyes of the artists with whom I've worked—whether you interview for a job, teach a new class, deliver a baby, or throw a baseball, performing challenges you in ways that can damage you both physically and psychologically.

When performers talk to me about performing, they describe how they engage. They tell me: "I sing with abandon," "It's as if I've shed my skin," "I perform as if I'm ad-libbing." They talk about going into a bubble, a zone, a flow. They are *in the moment*. They are just about "being."

These levels of self-expression and self-exposure that leave artists without the psychological armor necessary in everyday life is what performing is all about—this is what makes a performer a performing artist. I define this artistic phenomenon as a regression in the service of performing.

Stage Fright

Regression in the service of performing, although professionally organic and appropriate, can manifest itself in stage fright and become psychologically hazardous.

When performing, in order to fully commit to, connect to, and become totally immersed in their art, performers naturally let go of their unconscious, mental processes—the defense mechanisms that are used to ward off anxiety and that provide protection from unconscious feelings and memories, trauma, and conflicts. This leaves the artist emotionally vulnerable and raw while in performance. It can also render them actually unsafe and unprotected in the real world when they stop performing onstage.

Why?

Performers who experience unresolved, unconscious psychological conflict become overwhelmed by their defenselessness when in regression in the service of their art. These psychologically challenged artists unconsciously transfer their painful memories and trauma –stimulated by the material in their music, dance, or drama—onto the stage or into the pit. The performance aberrations, calamities, and mishaps are called stage fright. As you can imagine, stage fright brings many of these performers into my office.

REFLECTION 27

How much do you think about stage fright in your work?

1——2——3——4——5——6——7——8
1 being the lowest and 8 being the highest.

WHAT ARE YOU SEEING?

These performers describe physical experiences where their bodies freeze up, their hearts race or pound, their hands, knees, lips and voices shake, they experience dry mouth or a tight throat, have sweaty or cold hands, and nausea. Their bodies are going wild with cortisol and adrenaline, where they want to flee the performance and sometimes they even become violent. They also describe negative, pessimistic thoughts such as "I can't do this," "I have no business performing," "Everybody is going to find out how awful I am," "I'm going to make a fool of myself," "I'd better run." They have what's commonly known in the business as Imposter Syndrome. They are overwhelmed with fight-or-flight energy.

Over the years, I've identified two types of stage fright: chronic and acute.

Chronic stage fright is a constant fear of performing. These performers dread what they love. They often associate performing with an inability to breathe, move, think, or access any of their creative resources. *"I won't be able to tap into my creative self,"* is a common theme.

Stage fright can also be an acute experience, where performers are unexpectedly interrupted while performing work that is usually familiar and comfortable. Rather than a response to performing in general, this fright comes seemingly out of the blue.

The fight-or-flight response is fully engaged in both chronic and acute stage fright.

REFLECTION 28

How much chronic stage fright do you currently experience?

1——2——3——4——5——6——7——8

1 being the lowest and 8 being the highest.

WHAT ARE YOU SEEING?

How much acute stage fright do you currently experience?

1——2——3——4——5——6——7——8

1 being the lowest and 8 being the highest.

WHAT ARE YOU SEEING?

TABLEAU TEN: ISSY

Issy, a successful operatic coloratura, was referred to me years ago for short-term work by a psychiatrist who was treating her. Issy's psychiatrist knew that I worked exclusively with performers, with stage fright, and was familiar with the operatic repertoire. My work with Issy began with her anxious description of her performance experience.

"Even though I've sung 'The Queen of the Night' many times, I had a disastrous rehearsal period. It's strange. I'd be singing so well if I weren't exploding my usual spinning high F in both my arias. I don't understand it. I have my technique down. I'm terrified and have only four days until opening night."

Issy and I decided to meet daily.

"What, if anything, is unusual about this production?" I asked.

"Well, the sets are more elaborate, and that Maestro… if I could only follow the beat of that crazy Maestro."

"Crazy?" I asked.

"Yes. He flings his baton around. He let it fly during the orchestra dress and almost hit a violinist in her face. I become dizzy just watching him." She paused. "My head begins to pulse so loudly that I feel that my voice is being pounded out of me."

I had a choice. I could focus on the Maestro's alleged out of control behavior as Issy's projection or I could, as I did, inquire about her sensory references.

"What other times do you remember the sound of your head pulsing?"

"Oh…when my baby was born. When she let out her first scream, my head pulsed so loudly that I thought it would explode."

I took note of the repetition of the word explode.

"Oh, my God," Issy said with a gasp, "Uncle Alf! He told me if I screamed he'd kill me."

Through spurts of sobbing, Issy began to unfurl an early and hazy memory of being beaten until she bled when she was very young with what seemed to her like a "flying belt" by a deranged uncle. This event had been stored away and had not been consciously recalled, even in her ongoing psychiatric treatment.

Once the horror of Uncle Alf's assault was awakened and brought into consciousness, I used the "empty chair" technique to begin to work through her trauma. The empty chair technique is a Gestalt therapy exercise in which you express your thoughts and feelings as if you were talking to a specific person. This exercise was most cathartic for Issy and we decided to do some stage work in my office.

Issy sang her first aria on my office stage and when she came to her F she froze.

I paid attention to my intuition and remembered the curse that haunted her "Magic Flute" arias.

I asked Issy if she was aware that many singers think that Der Hollé Racher and O Tsit-tre Nicht sound like screaming if not performed exceptionally well.

"I know," she once again gasped. "They're known as killers of the voice."

Because of Issy's familiarity with the therapeutic process, she quickly put the pieces together.

She whispered, "I'd feel in mortal danger if I were to scream my high F in the face of this crazy Maestro's baton."

"You were in great danger if you had screamed with Uncle Alf," I responded. "However, not even these killer arias or your crazed conductor can put you in that kind of danger now." Bringing Issy into her present artistic reality, I said, "You may be at risk of getting poor reviews, but Issy, your physical being is not in jeopardy today."

In our final session, I asked Issy to explode the operatic mythology that had contributed to her stage fright by helping her change her thinking each time she felt overwhelmed by her traumatic past. And she came up with: "I can sing the hell out of these arias. I am The Queen of the Night."

Issy received fantastic reviews!

Because performers regress on the stage or in the pit, the phobic reaction, and as in Issy's case, the unexpected disruption, both known as stage fright, are responses to past trauma. Each is triggered by a specific dramatic or musical event that holds some unconscious meaning for them. The performer's dread, anxiety, and panic are signals that old trauma is about to emerge. This awareness overwhelms the performer. I have found that the way they manifest their fright is through resurrection and reenactment of the trauma.

REFLECTION 29

What triggers your stage fright?

WHAT ARE YOU SEEING?

I believe that attempts to overcome both chronic and acute stage fright—meditation, imaging, affirmation, or beta-blockers—provide only temporary or minimal relief, as the underlying causes are not being addressed.

When performers understand how regression in the service of performing organically affects them, they need not be surprised when they experience what they call stage fright. They can resolve the material that has become conscious when regressed and once again engage with their art.

When performers become aware that *stage fright is not a fear of the stage*, they can accept that it is part of the artistic process and learn to deal with it, onstage and off, in ways that allow them to realize their performance potential.

When I hear performers in my office say: I can keep on performing," "I have my love back," "The stage is my friend," "The stage is my home again," I know that these performers understand that stage fright is not a fear of the stage.

Addiction

"Here's to fame and fortune," Victor proclaimed ebulliently as he prepared to read his review in my office.

Oh, be careful what you wish for, I thought to myself!

Regardless of the differences between actors, dancers, musicians and vocal artists, the addictive nature of performing affects the performance potential of all performing artists to some degree. They come in to talk with me when this constant craving to be acknowledged and validated—a cultural value—brings such great distress that it becomes unmanageable.

Some of the performers who come to see me have developed a dependency on whatever their audience deems to bestow upon them, be it applause, critical acclaim and the love or riches that *might* follow. They tell me, "It's like I'm chemically addicted."

The audience plays its own significant role during every live performance. It provides performers with a special energy that serves as a primary source of the performer's adrenaline. Performers play off this energy. When an artist has a good audience, the satisfaction on both sides of the proscenium allows everybody to exit the theatre happy. It is a constructive symbiosis.

Yet, artists tell me about times when they've performed their hearts out, only to be greeted by lukewarm clapping, shabbily dressed, snoring, candy-wrapper-crumpling audiences. Their heartbreak is understandable as questions like, "What do I have to do?" come up in our sessions. They tell me how insecure and uncertain their relationship with their audience feels. When a performer has a bad audience, it's like a bad parent/child fit: It can be devastating.

How very psychologically hazardous the audience/performer relationship can be to performance potential! This is particularly true for performers who are hooked on applause. It's as if audience applause were a drug fueling their self-esteem — or not!

REFLECTION 30

How addicted are you to praise?

1——2——3——4——5——6——7——8
1 being the lowest and 8 being the highest.

WHAT ARE YOU SEEING?

The audience, of course, is part of a greater addiction, the performer's public: fans, critics, social media followers, voyeurs, interested or not. So begins the dance. Often the public has grandiose and impractical expectations that propel performers into nearly schizophrenic efforts to fulfill whatever images the public imposes. When the public doesn't approve of an artist, in performance or in his personal life, and the artist longs for their adoration, he or she can lose a sense of self. Many performers, famous or not, sacrifice personal authenticity. When they rely on their public for their identity, self-loathing, victimization and shame emerge, manifesting in dis-graceful conduct.

The addictive nature of show business takes advantage of a performer's ambition to perform and become famous. The smell of that grease paint seduces many "wannabes" as well as veterans in the business. They become so obsessed with the roar of the crowd that they often prostitute themselves. Although it is often to pay the bills, they take ridiculous roles in commercials to be seen. They take gigs that they know they're not suited for and ultimately, they don't show up well and get bad reviews. They go on the road when it's bad for their families. They back-stab fellow performers. There is a common expression in the business that *he or she slept his way to the top*—some succumb to that cultural icon, the casting couch. No stakes seem too high.

REFLECTION 31

How often do you betray yourself for adoration and promotion?

1——2——3——4——5——6——7——8
1 being the lowest and 8 being the highest.

WHAT ARE YOU SEEING?

Some performers long to be visible and invisible at the same time. This internal battle to be seen and unseen torments many performing artists and interferes with the realization of their performance potential. They experience unbearable ambivalence. They want to be seen and known, yet they hate the paparazzi. They want their photograph everywhere, yet they yearn for privacy. They crave anonymity, yet they want to be bigger than life. These dichotomies come at great cost to their professional and personal lives.

REFLECTION 32

Circle the choices you might be making

You avoid the "paparazzi" *or* You want to be seen and known

You desire privacy *or* You want your photograph everywhere

You want to be anonymous *or* You want to be bigger than life

WHAT ARE YOU SEEING?

As with any addiction, music-making, singing, dancing, and acting can feel like a narcotic. And when not performing, cravings develop. Many artists don't know what to do with themselves with their downtime. In our sessions, performers have described times between engagements as dry spells. They refer to their "emotional DTs."

Some performers, when not working, have injured themselves with excessive practice. This behavior, which I consider dissonant, is called "overuse syndrome" by the medical community. Many performers additionally turn to retail therapy or substance abuse.

Between gigs is *waiting time*, and although they audition, practice and train, performers reveal performance-defeating thoughts such as, "I'll never work again" or "I don't understand why I didn't get the gig" or even "I'm gonna quit."

It's a very psychologically hazardous time when performing is all they want to do. Every time a gig ends, a weaning period begins, triggering anxiety, depression, and a sense of helplessness and hopelessness. And then they win a job and it's a fix. This addictive business of show can be an exhausting cycle. And that's show biz.

Rejection
Performing threatens performance potential in yet another way.

Too loud

Not enough

Too old

Went another way

Already cast

Not enough experience

NO

REFLECTION 33

What do you feel when you hear these words?

WHAT ARE YOU SEEING?

Rejection is the most predictable part of performing. It is an integral and expected aspect of the performing process. Yet, when performers are not chosen, many feel worthless and undeserving.

How true is this for you?

Even though performing artists are aware that you either get the gig or you don't — when they aren't cast, don't win a chair, don't get the solo, or when the star does not go up on the dressing room door — performers frequently become depressed or anxious, and can feel scorned and even righteously indignant. And, since every artist strives to have a signature style, professional judgment by coaches, choreographers, conductors, directors, and critics, particularly in auditions, when notes are given in rehearsals, or in reviews, is interpreted as personal rejection. They come into my office defeated, dejected and demoralized saying:

"I'll never work again."

"My life is a waste."

"I have no control over my life."

"What made me think I even had a chance?"

"I must be a horrible person."

REFLECTION 34

How much do you feel rejected in your work?

1——2——3——4——5——6——7——8

1 being the lowest and 8 being the highest.

WHAT ARE YOU SEEING?

TABLEAU ELEVEN: MARIE

It was two years into her therapy before I learned that Marie, a French Horn player, was a cutter.

"I can deal with this pain and I am in control," she said, as she showed me the tiny gashes on her legs.

Marie and I agreed that it was indeed wonderful to have such control over something in her life. She'd felt so helpless and so rejected in her work life that the pain of cutting herself paled in comparison to the pain of rejection she was experiencing.

The change in her thinking was, could she be in control of something that was pleasurable rather than painful?

That was our work. We met twice a week over the next couple of months to consider together what she might find pleasurable, given that she could not control professional rejection. During this time Marie met with my consulting psycho-pharmacologist who recommended that Marie begin a protocol of SSRIs, which helped her immensely.

In therapy, Marie decided that she would rather be in control of pleasure than pain, and she chose to learn to sing. She determined that whenever she had the impulse to cut herself to gain control, she would call me instead of acting on her impulse and using the small knife to inflict pain. She would leave a message every time she felt the urge to cut; she didn't have to talk to me, she just had to call me and sing into the phone, which gave her a lot of pleasure. The singing changed her brain chemistry. She eventually stopped cutting and, as she began thinking differently about rejection, Marie began to work.

REFLECTION 35

How often do you self-harm because of rejection?

1——2——3——4——5——6——7——8
1 being the lowest and 8 being the highest.

WHAT ARE YOU SEEING?

"I give up my whole life to perform."

The preparation and attention that performing demands can easily take over an artist's entire life. Prior to stepping onto a stage or into a pit, actors, dancers, musicians, and vocal artists, are required to study, practice, coach, travel, audition, rehearse, and promote themselves. Even veterans of the business easily spend all their time and energy on their work. As a result, many performers don't or can't invest in or depend on personal relationships or anything else since they have so little to give in return.

REFLECTION 36

*How much time and energy do you devote to activities
and/or relationships outside your work life?*

1——2——3——4——5——6——7——8
1 being the lowest and 8 being the highest.

WHAT ARE YOU SEEING?

TABLEAU TWELVE: ELAINE

Elaine, a very successful white female actor with whom I've worked for several years, couldn't win an audition to save her soul. "They're going ethnic, they're going ethnic," she kept repeating, "and I'm not working. I can't not work. I understand it. But I'm afraid. I want everyone to work but the rejection is killing me. I'm so confused. I don't want to sound like a racist and I'm drinking too much and I'm beginning to hate myself."

Elaine spoke to the huge racial chasm in her profession.

She maintained her industry was creating racial competition and alienation and was doing nothing to bridge the conflict to unite the artists in supporting one another. Unfortunately, I was unable able to help Elaine look within to explore her personal thoughts, feelings, and history about rejection. Elaine not only left therapy but she stopped acting and is seeking a managerial position.

I am searching myself to understand whether I, too, was rejecting Elaine. I found it challenging to listen to her inner life and stay away from racial content, as I do not yet know how to be emotionally detached in the therapy room during this time of racial reckoning.

Performing can cause many artists to feel unlikable and even unlovable. Who doesn't recall Sally Field's acceptance speech as she received her Oscar many years ago? "I can't deny the fact that you like me, right now, you like me." These doubts impact the performer's self-esteem, the ways they interact with their colleagues, with their families, with their public and, of course, their performance potential.

REFLECTION 37

How much does performing define you?

1——2——3——4——5——6——7——8
1 being the lowest and 8 being the highest.

WHAT ARE YOU SEEING?

MOURNING

One of the most psychologically hazardous aspects of performing, and therefore one of the most devastating to the artist's performance potential, is the never-ending flow of nightly curtains, exits, and final chords. Intangible moments of creativity are the sole yield of a performer's labor. These moments of sound, sight, and motion can be preserved only by technology or revived by the memory of the muscle, the senses or the heart. Each moment brings exhilaration rarely to be equaled. The death of the same moment brings despair: the ecstasy and the agony. Performers are constantly experiencing attachment and loss.

Performing keeps them forever mourning.

And Cole Porter's lyrics come floating up: "Every Time I Say Goodbye, I die a little."

However glorious it is for those who set foot on a stage, slip on a ballet slipper, hold a mike or touch the ivory keys, performing artists need to be aware that psychological hazards are intrinsic in their culture and that they are performing at their own psychological risk—risking the realization of their performance potential, onstage and off.

PERFORMER PERSONALITY PROFILES

Before I introduce you to the Performer Personality Profiles that I observed, defined and classified over my many years working with performing artists, I invite you to contemplate the names of the four personalities:

Problem-Ridden Performer

Pugnacious Performer

Promising Performer

Potential-Realized Performer

REFLECTION 38

At this moment in time, what about each name resonates with and reflects you?

WHAT ARE YOU SEEING?

These profiles articulate and clarify both what is preventing you from reaching your performance potential and what empowers you to realize it.

Before you become acquainted with the four personalities, it's important that you understand the concept of energy, as I define it in my practice, as energy is the foundation of the personality profiles.

ENERGY

Energy is composed of *thoughts* (ideas, beliefs, reasoning, perceptions, intuition, and insight); *brain hormones* (adrenaline, cortisol, dopamine, and oxytocin); *feelings* (physical sensations: jitters, butterflies, headaches, stomach aches); *emotions* (mad, sad, glad, scared, and associated affects); *characteristics* (curiosity, confidence, civility, creativity, etc.) and *performance* (action, interaction, behavior, patterns of being and behaving, facial communication, and physical demeanor).

Energy fluctuates, like a musical scale… it goes up and down, and the tempi can move very quickly.

**Think about a time you performed well—
a song, a monologue, a presentation, a riff, any task—
and compare it to another time when you
didn't perform the same activity as well.**

What was different?

REFLECTION 39

How much did your energy fluctuate when you performed well?

1——2——3——4——5——6——7——8

1 being the lowest and 8 being the highest.

WHAT ARE YOU SEEING?

How much did your energy fluctuate when you didn't perform well?

1——2——3——4——5——6——7——8

1 being the lowest and 8 being the highest.

WHAT ARE YOU SEEING?

These experiences are why it's important to understand energy.

Why?

You can control your own energy; energy needn't fluctuate and change. Your performances—ways of showing up, ways of being and behaving—needn't be inconsistent.

Any change in energy affects how you perform therefore creating the impressions and perceptions that others form about you. However beware, for there are two types of energy: harmonic and dissonant. Harmonic energy empowers performance potential, dissonant energy prevents it.

Harmonic Energy

Harmony is defined as the combination of simultaneously sounded musical notes to produce chords having a pleasing effect. Indeed, the very word harmony—say it aloud: HAR-MO-NY—is musical and pleasing to the ear. Harmony is also a desirable state of being.

One way to define harmony and understand *harmonic energy* is to think of someone in your life whom you love to be around. Are you remembering experiences of wanting to be near this person? Being inspired by them? Wanting to be a part of their success? You might even remember being subtly changed by them.

Write five words that describe how this person shows up.

1.

2.

3.

4.

5.

Supportive, optimistic, exhilarating, fun, calm, kind, helpful, fearless, friendly, confident, joyful, passionate, expressive, curious, intuitive, generous, caring, purposeful, present, directed, creative, professional, positive, empowering and aware.

How many of these words showed up on your list?

How much do you recognize yourself in these traits?

> *"Smiling isn't hard work… make the shape with*
> *your face and the rest takes care of itself."*
>
> "CALL THE MIDWIFE"

When you show up with harmonic energy, you have great eye contact, a memorable and contagious smile, laughing eyes, good hygiene, make-up that is applied to reflect who you are—your self-care and self-respect are apparent. Physical attributes—the way you hold your head, your posture, your handshake—make a rainy day feel sunny.

Harmonic energy is based on a strong sense of yourself; on conscious awareness of *who* you are. You are aligned with *what* you do and *how* you do it. The more you know who you are, the more harmonic energy is available.

Harmonic energy releases creative hormones: serotonin, dopamine and oxytocin, the love and social bonding hormone; hormones that connect you with your audiences and with your colleagues. Harmonic energy is healing, growth-oriented and empowering.

Harmonic energy empowers performance potential.

REFLECTION 40

How much harmonic energy are you currently experiencing and expressing?

1——2——3——4——5——6——7——8

1 being the lowest and 8 being the highest.

WHAT ARE YOU SEEING?

Dissonant Energy

If you are disappointed with your level of harmonic energy, chances are you're experiencing *dissonant energy*. With dissonant energy, you are unable to reach your performance potential.

One way to understand *dissonant energy* is to think about someone who exhausts and depletes you. You are perhaps recalling experiences with people who distract and drain you; folks who are just no fun to be around. People who are always in overwhelm, in crisis, because they are constantly under pressure… always stressed out. They exhibit *"It's all about me"* ways of showing up in the world. And you want to run for the hills!

Write five words that describe how this person shows up.

1.

2.

3.

4.

5.

How many of the following words showed up on your list?

Self-centered, judgmental, stuck, accusatory, boring, complaining, distracted, exhausting, overwhelmed, apathetic, conflicted, struggling, resistant, argumentative, negative, victimized, and controlling.

This is dissonant energy.
How much do you recognize yourself in these traits?

REFLECTION 41

How much dissonant energy are you currently
experiencing and expressing?

1——2——3——4——5——6——7——8
1 being the lowest and 8 being the highest.

WHAT ARE YOU SEEING?

Many performers with whom I've worked used their harmonic energy to realize their *possibility*—that greatness that they have within. They were empowered.

However, many others were not. These performers were talking to me because they were *not* realizing their performance potential.

"Why am I not achieving it?"

These performers were feeling bad about themselves both professionally and personally.

As I listened to them over the years, one word kept circulating in my mind. That word was DIVA. And I have been writing and lecturing about diva patterns for more than thirty years. Think about the *diva*.

What kinds of thoughts, feelings, characteristics and
behaviors does the diva bring to mind for you?

Here are some of my thoughts and discoveries.

The word "diva" came into the English language in the late 19th century. Historically, in Italian, a *diva* was a female deity. Today, the diva and *divo* are mortals with potential god-like abilities. F. Paul Driscoll of Opera News wrote about Aretha Franklin, "Franklin's most popular nickname was "The Queen," a fitting title for a woman who ruled every stage on which she stood with absolute power. But for me, Franklin defined the concept of "diva" — the artist as a goddess.

Today, divas are associated with celebrities and luminaries who transport and inspire us to honor *our* diva within.

Yet, many divas have fallen from grace.

Today, the diva is much more synonymous with the devil than with the divine. This realization, as early as the 1980s, led me to identify a condition that I call *the diva syndrome.*

THE DIVA SYNDROME

A dissonant energy-filled condition that prevents performers from realizing their performance potential.

the diva syndrome is composed of fight-or-flight, outcome-focused, impossibility-driven, personalization, and distorted feeling patterns.

Fight-or-flight patterns predominate in *the diva syndrome.*

Fight-or-flight thoughts, feelings, characteristics, and behaviors are emergency, survival, panic, and crisis patterns that originally came from a place of real and present physical danger. These are motivated in response to stimuli that create a false sense of emergency where some flee and others attack. Fight-or-flight keeps them focused on survival. Both have very unhealthy physical and psychological effects. The fight-or-flight response is fueled by adrenaline and cortisol which, if experienced for long periods of time, kills off healthy cells in the body.

Fear and anger are major derivative affects of flight-or-fight. Shame, embarrassment, envy, and rage are additional emotional outgrowths. Dissonant energy generated by fear and anger-based reactions makes it impossible to reach performance potential.

REFLECTION 42

How much do you experience fight-or-flight patterns?

1——2——3——4——5——6——7——8

1 being the lowest and 8 being the highest.

WHAT ARE YOU SEEING?

Outcome patterns are a dominant piece of *the diva syndrome*.

One way of approaching performance is to focus on results—on what's going to happen and how each performance will end. Outcome, results, or product patterns are filled with dissonant energy as they are problem-focused, fixated on mistakes and flaws, mired in past imperfections and in anticipated future difficulties. The past cannot be changed, and when you think about it, the future is really a figment of your imagination. Therefore, when focused on past and future you are not in the moment, not in the now, not in the flow, not in the day—out of control of your performance. Many performers believe that they have to think about technique when they perform. However, this too breaks the flow. They also think that they have to be perfect, which of course takes the artist out of their performance piece. Both technique and perfection are outcome thoughts. When an outcome or a result is decided upon and the focus of a performance remains on that outcome, rather than on how to realize that outcome, performance potential cannot be reached.

REFLECTION 43

How much do you focus on outcome and results in performance?

1——2——3——4——5——6——7——8
1 being the lowest and 8 being the highest.

WHAT ARE YOU SEEING?

**Impossibility-driven patterns are an
integral part of *the diva syndrome*.**

When you find it impossible to see the opportunities and possibilities in any situation, event, circumstance, person or place, you are paralyzed by your dissonant energy. Envisioning what you *won't do, shouldn't do, can't do,* paradoxically, is a guarantee that you *won't* reach your performance potential.

REFLECTION 44

How driven are you by the impossible?

1——2——3——4——5——6——7——8
1 being the lowest and 8 being the highest.

WHAT ARE YOU SEEING?

**Taking everything personally is a critical
pattern of *the diva syndrome*.**

With personalization, thoughts, feelings, characteristics, and behaviors, everything and anything is personal. Everything and anything causes personal insult and injury. These perceived affronts prevent the realization of performance potential as they reinforce and give power to the other *diva syndrome* patterns and create a toxic *diva syndrome* cycle.

REFLECTION 45

To what extent do you take things personally?

1——2——3——4——5——6——7——8
1 being the lowest and 8 being the highest.

WHAT ARE YOU SEEING?

Two feeling patterns are rampant in *the diva syndrome.* Both patterns are magical thinking. These feeling patterns involve the belief that feelings have powers that they do not possess and when acted upon prevent the realization of performance potential.

The first feeling pattern is the belief that feelings are facts. Emotional lives do not define truth or actuality. When accepted as such, they cause confusion and chaos as well as complicate communication and personal relatedness. When choices and decisions are based on feelings, then consensual validation—that which is commonly accepted—becomes distorted. Our emotional lives are not barometers for reality.

REFLECTION 46

How often do you act on the belief that your feelings are facts?

1——2——3——4——5——6——7——8
1 being the lowest and 8 being the highest.

WHAT ARE YOU SEEING?

The second feeling pattern is the belief that you can make somebody else feel. Each one of us is responsible for our own emotional lives only. When you endow yourself with a power that you do not have, your self-esteem is falsely inflated with abilities that are not real. We can want someone else to feel something, but the choice of whether they feel it or not is theirs. I can love you with all my heart, but I can't make you love me back. I may want to hurt your feelings, but only you can choose whether or not to feel hurt.

REFLECTION 47

How often do you act on the belief that you can make someone else feel?

1——2——3——4——5——6——7——8
1 being the lowest and 8 being the highest.

WHAT ARE YOU SEEING?

When you let these ubiquitous feeling patterns dominate and dictate how you think and how you behave, you will be mired in *the diva syndrome*.

REFLECTION 48

How much do you recognize diva syndrome patterns in yourself?

1——2——3——4——5——6——7——8
1 being the lowest and 8 being the highest.

WHAT ARE YOU SEEING?

How much do you recognize diva syndrome patterns in your family, friends and colleagues?

1——2——3——4——5——6——7——8
1 being the lowest and 8 being the highest.

WHAT ARE YOU SEEING?

As you hold Hamlet's mirror, you may see yourself in these patterns, feel the dissonant energy and become aware that you are suffering *the diva syndrome*. The first two performer personalities, The Problem-Ridden and Pugnacious Performer, will give you insight that will help you understand what's preventing you from reaching your performance potential. At the same time, you may catch sight of how you can realize that possibility that you hold within, shift into harmonic energy and move beyond these personalities to become a Promising or Potential-Realized Performer.

THE PROBLEM-RIDDEN PERFORMER PERSONALITY PROFILE

The Problem-Ridden Performer feels the excruciating pain of *the diva syndrome*'s performance-defeating and self-destructive patterns of being and behaving.

I know from my work that they often feel undeserving and experience severe self-doubt and self-loathing. Performers in this profile are inundated with overwhelming dissonant energy.

They use more muscles to frown than to smile. Their demeanor, their posture, their lack of eye contact, their manner of dress, the way they put themselves together, their hygiene—how they literally face the world—reflects their dissonant energy. They show up wounded, defensive, withdrawn, and of course, always stressed out.

REFLECTION 49

How often do you frown?

1——2——3——4——5——6——7——8
1 being the lowest and 8 being the highest.

WHAT ARE YOU SEEING?

How often do you make eye contact?

1——2——3——4——5——6——7——8
1 being the lowest and 8 being the highest.

WHAT ARE YOU SEEING?

Quotes I've heard in my office from Problem-Ridden Performers include:

"I'm so ashamed."

"I don't deserve anything good."

"I feel like nobody cares about me."

"My audiences hate me."

"I'm such a loser."

"I work so hard to make the corps like me."

"Why bother?"

Life is unfair."

"Success is not possible for me."

"I give up."

"The whole world thinks I don't have a real job. I guess I don't!"

"Did I say the wrong thing?"

"I was so mad I decided to quit."

"Why even try when I don't stand a chance to win the gig."

"I'm to blame."

"I want a drink."

"I want to stay under the covers all day and hide."

"I'm a fraud and soon everyone will know it."

Problem-Ridden Performers are adamant that they are at the effect of their histories, at the mercy of everything in their lives. They resolutely believe they have no choice, no options, and no possibilities. They're certain that they are under the power of the bullies of the world and unfair competition. Their constant complaints reflect their sense of victimization. They suffer, and the world knows it. They vomit up their problems, ad nauseam. Problem-Ridden Performers have no boundaries. I've found that they revel in their problems and believe that they give them security, as their suffering is their only true and constant knowledge base.

Problem-Ridden Performers show up with *diva syndrome* attitudes of "Everything is personal." "Everything happens to me." This thinking creates problematic behavior: addictions, lying, showing-up late, unprepared, not showing up at all… not performing, not working—all about problems, problems, problems.

Life is a Sisyphean effort: the Greek God spent his life pushing a rock up a mountain only to have it roll back onto him, precipitating his fall. The rock was too heavy and the mountain too steep. Repetitive pushing and climbing seemed to be Sisyphus's only option. Such is the life of many Problem-Ridden Performers.

REFLECTION 50

How often do you feel abused?

1——2——3——4——5——6——7——8
1 being the lowest and 8 being the highest.

WHAT ARE YOU SEEING?

Problem-Ridden Performers are convinced that they can't do anything right because they have no control: "Life holds a personal grudge against me." The only way that many of these performers can make sense of their plight is to feel unworthy. Feelings dominate and dictate the way these performers behave. Feelings drive their choices and doom them to be victims.

REFLECTION 51

How much do you think that you're a victim?

1——2——3——4——5——6——7——8
1 being the lowest and 8 being the highest.

WHAT ARE YOU SEEING?

These performers do express conviction. But their ability to assert themselves is used to declare their powerlessness and shame. These convictions, filled with dissonant energy, propel their work. Problem-Ridden Performers are unmotivated and uninspired to see the possibilities and the opportunities available to them or anyone else. They resist any success or greatness.

Let me tell you about a violist I'll call Dorothy.

Dorothy sat in the last chair of her orchestra. She had tenure—surprisingly, not because of her abundant musical abilities but because of her dissonant energy and behavior. When she entered therapy, Dorothy had been fined by her union and at that time was being warned of more severe penalties. I believe that's what brought her into therapy, although I have never been quite certain.

TABLEAU THIRTEEN: DOROTHY

Dorothy came into my office and as she sat on my light blue ultra-suede couch she spilled her cup of coffee. It also burnt her. "Ouch," she said, "I'm so sorry. Now I'm going to make you hate me too. I wouldn't blame you if you wouldn't see me—I mess up everything." Tears rolled down her cheeks.

This was our first session. I sat and waited. My intuition told me not to hand Dorothy a tissue, but to ignore this behavior. I sensed that she wanted me to hate her, which would reward her actions.

Dorothy was one of seven children. She was waiting for the world to give her the attention and comfort that she had never been given at home. She did manage to get attention as an adult. However, her conduct was self-defeating and the attention negative.

"It's not fair," she cried, "my mother didn't even put me to bed at night."

It's true, it wasn't fair. However, if Dorothy was going to hold on to her world-view—"the world of the unjust"—as she referred to it, nothing was going to change for her.

Dorothy and I explored her victimization. She described that whenever she entered her orchestra pit she would have accidents, and the other musicians would be mean to her... "the world of the unjust!"

"I feel so guilty… I guess I'd be mean to me too. But I try so hard. I've been warned twice that If I'm late again, I'll be put on probation, even after I explained that I'm so, so sorry. I guess I deserve to be fired. Thank God for tenure."

After about six years, Dorothy began to feel uncomfortable with negative attention; it was no longer serving her. Dorothy realized that the only way that she had felt powerful was believing that she could control people's negative feelings and responses toward her by being unprofessional and careless. She almost took pride and comfort in her victimization and it was only after she became aware that she could not make other people feel, that her real therapy began. She started learning self-care and how to comfort herself. She also began to take responsibility for her self-pitying and fatalistic attitudes, as well as her self-sabotaging behavior.

Over the course of her fifteen-year therapy, which is not a long therapy with her level of Divanesque patterns, Dorothy understood that the world would not give her the parenting she craved, and that she needed to work through her feelings of loss and anger instead of acting them out.

Over the years, as Dorothy began to recognize and accept her wonderful personal and professional attributes, she also became aware of her faulty thinking and what caused people to be so nasty to her. "I wanted people to punish me so that the first people (who by that time were deceased) who caused me pain might notice and take care of me," she said in amazement. At that point, she began coming to rehearsals prepared, on time and with a more collegial spirit. At the same time, she realized that she had wanted me, in particular, to clean up her messes.

Dorothy's therapy became filled with tears of awareness and I began handing her tissues.

Dorothy was lucky and did the work she needed to do; many Problem-Ridden Performers flee therapy feeling victimized by the therapeutic process.

The Problem-Ridden Performer lives on the precipice of survival. *The diva syndrome's* flight energy is reflected by apathy, indecisiveness, and unprofessionalism. These performers think about running away to fantasized safety. They flee from imagined threats such as, "They think I'm too fat," "They think I'm terrible," and "They hate me." Flight is perceived as self-preservation. However, for most, fleeing causes them to be self-absorbed and ungenerous, which naturally pushes others away.

REFLECTION 52

How much are you currently hiding?

1——2——3——4——5——6——7——8
1 being the lowest and 8 being the highest.

WHAT ARE YOU SEEING?

Problem-Ridden Performers' core feeling is fear. And when they do not flee, they are consumed with fear and dissonant energy. These performers are so very anxious about the future and so very worried about the past. When they do engage and perform, they're unenthusiastic and pessimistic. Many experience stage fright. Another form of showing up that many find difficult is decision-making. And if choices are made, they are fear-driven. However, most flee; they don't do anything! They withdraw and avoid. *They don't perform!*

REFLECTION 53

How much fear are you currently experiencing?

1——2——3——4——5——6——7——8
1 being the lowest and 8 being the highest.

WHAT ARE YOU SEEING?

How much do you avoid?

1——2——3——4——5——6——7——8
1 being the lowest and 8 being the highest.

WHAT ARE YOU SEEING?

The three Ds, despair, doubt, and desperation, also populate the emotional lives of the Problem-Ridden Performer. Depression , a fourth D, is also common, depleting their self-esteem even more. Guilt about things they've done or said leads them to second-guess themselves, particularly in their work. And since these performers unbendingly believe that everything is their fault, they are without self-forgiveness, causing them to apologize profusely and constantly, annoying everyone around them. They are racked with shame.

REFLECTION 54

How much do you apologize?

1——2——3——4——5——6——7——8
1 being the lowest and 8 being the highest.

WHAT ARE YOU SEEING?

REFLECTION 55

How much of each emotion do you currently see in yourself?

Despair

1——2——3——4——5——6——7——8
1 being the lowest and 8 being the highest.

WHAT ARE YOU SEEING?

Doubt

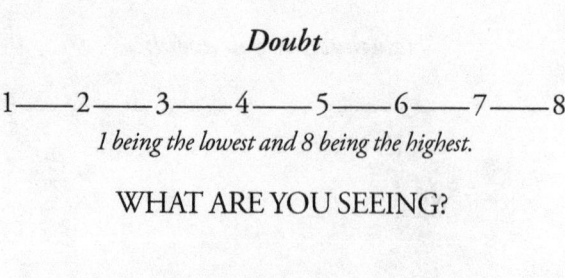

1——2——3——4——5——6——7——8
1 being the lowest and 8 being the highest.

WHAT ARE YOU SEEING?

Desperation

1——2——3——4——5——6——7——8
1 being the lowest and 8 being the highest.

WHAT ARE YOU SEEING?

Depression

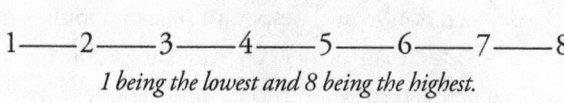

1——2——3——4——5——6——7——8
1 being the lowest and 8 being the highest.

WHAT ARE YOU SEEING?

Guilt

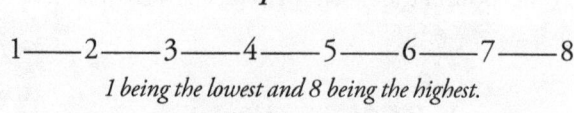

1——2——3——4——5——6——7——8
1 being the lowest and 8 being the highest.

WHAT ARE YOU SEEING?

Shame

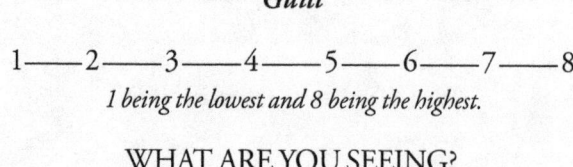

1——2——3——4——5——6——7——8
1 being the lowest and 8 being the highest.

WHAT ARE YOU SEEING?

The diva syndrome's outcome-focused patterns are dramatically evident in those who see themselves in The Problem-Ridden Performer Personality.

Outcome-focused thoughts that I have heard in my office include:

"I will be horrible."

"I will make so many mistakes."

"My agent will dump me."

"Everything will go wrong."

"I'll look fat."

"I won't hit that note."

"I'll go up on my lines."

"This performance will ruin my career."

I found in my work that because outcome patterns are so filled with dissonant energy, and because these performers are intensely focused on results; they futurize, thus making it impossible for them to stay in the performance moment.

In order to satisfy their dissonant, self-fulfilling outcome, they sabotage their work efforts and think about technique when they perform. I believe that thinking about technique in performance is like thinking about the alphabet when spelling a word. It breaks up the flow. Many performers with whom I've worked believe that they have to be perfect, which of course takes the artistry out of their performance piece. Others procrastinate, ensuring that they won't realize their performance potential. Technique, perfection, and procrastination are outcome thoughts and distract everyone from being in the now.

REFLECTION 56

How much do you try to achieve perfection?

1——2——3——4——5——6——7——8
1 being the lowest and 8 being the highest.

WHAT ARE YOU SEEING?

How much do you procrastinate?

1——2——3——4——5——6——7——8
1 being the lowest and 8 being the highest.

WHAT ARE YOU SEEING?

It's understandable that Problem-Ridden Performers think that they're invisible, unacknowledged and without a voice.

Is it any wonder that they are unable to realize their performance potential? Most resist changing their thinking, can only take things personally, and are incapable of seeing their gifts and taking advantage of their opportunities. They are truly suffering "the slings and arrows" of the dissonant-filled *diva syndrome*.

REFLECTION 57

How much do you currently identify with
The Problem-Ridden Performer Personality?

1——2——3——4——5——6——7——8
1 being the lowest and 8 being the highest.

WHAT ARE YOU SEEING?

THE PUGNACIOUS PERFORMER
PERSONALITY PROFILE

Although Pugnacious Performers exhibit slightly more harmonic energy than Problem-Ridden Performers, they also suffer *the diva syndrome*. How does this increase in harmonic energy impact their performance potential? Amazingly, it enables many to perform, and to perform well. Why? Pugnacious Performers get a lot accomplished. They move forward in their performance lives as one-shot wonders thanks to adrenaline, willpower, bullying and intimidation, often with extraordinary, short-term results.

TABLEAU FOURTEEN: SABRINA

Sabrina marched into my office, looked around, and sat in my chair. This was a first. I have an ergonomic chair in my office as I have back problems, and my chair has been a godsend. I took a seat on my therapy couch.

"Of course I'm angry. I'm only in here because that director is making me, he's envious that I know more than he does. What does he want me to do, not tell him when he misses the mark and stay in his stupid rehearsals?" To Sabrina, her feelings were fact and she acted on them. She needed to be right.

Sabrina then began by telling me that she was an over-sexed child stimulated by a lesbian mother who left home when Sabrina was ten. Sabrina was left with a very disturbed obsessive father who would have fits of rage at Sabrina and her two siblings, George and Henry.

"I started acting at seven and it saved my life. I know much more than most of my directors and it really irritates them. As you can tell, I'm extremely intelligent."

And indeed, she was.

Although Sabrina was in demand, directors were finding her difficult to work with. Sabrina believed that her director's "prompting" to seek therapy was the function of envy and asked me what I thought.

Sabrina proceeded to inform me about what I was thinking. She was quite psychologically knowledgeable about herself and her life, and we continued to talk about what she thought was in my head for some time.

Sabrina not only needed to be director of her life, she also needed to be in control of her therapy. If she ever thought that I was becoming directive or authoritative, she would angrily storm out of the session and return for our next scheduled meeting without acknowledging her dismissive, bullying behavior. And this pattern continued for many months until she began to realize that I did not want or need to control her. She acted out in the therapy room until she saw that one, I didn't give a damn, and two, that her need to be right wasn't serving her. Sabrina was creative and curious enough to see what was going on.

"I trust you," she said, "because you don't challenge my 'runs,'" as she referred to her aggressive actions. And our work began. Sabrina also voluntarily began sitting on my therapy couch, giving me back my chair. She would later tell me I could give her "notes."

Sabrina not only changed in my office, she changed in her rehearsal studios as well. She became more collegial with her directors, realizing that art, like therapy, is a collaboration. Sabrina is now a well-known presence both on film and stage, highly recognized for portraying evil characters. We remain very close.

The personality of the Pugnacious Performer is characterized by entitlement and grandiosity, by bullying and arrogance, and an attitude of "I'm God's gift to the world," which exhausts, drains and alienates others.

If you are seeing yourself in the personality of the Pugnacious Performer, you know that your performance potential can seem unlimited—until it isn't, and that you work until you thunderously fall. You perform until the dissonant-filled *diva syndrome* overwhelms you.

Unlike performers in the first profile who manifest a flight mentality,

Pugnacious Performers have a fight mentality. Like performers in the first profile, their dissonant energy is also emergency energy—survival, panic, and crisis energy—fueled by adrenaline and cortisol. However, their adrenaline can serve as a short-term fix in actual emergencies onstage and off, such as: on-set accidents, performing with a fever or when injured, or dealing with a sick child. But fight energy is not sustainable. It is so active and intense that if experienced for too long, it can be fatal.

Unlike Problem-Ridden Performers whose core feeling is fear, Pugnacious Performers' core feeling is *anger*. They have temper-tantrums, hissy-fits, rage reactions, and explosive melt-downs. No one in their environment is immune. These performers don't veer from decision-making, however, most of their choices are anger-driven.

REFLECTION 58

How often do you experience out of control anger?

1——2——3——4——5——6——7——8
1 being the lowest and 8 being the highest.

WHAT ARE YOU SEEING?

These performers find conflict in everything. They almost desperately *need* struggle in their lives. They are controlling and competitive and show up as very defiant and aggressive.

REFLECTION 59

How much do you need conflict in your life?

1——2——3——4——5——6——7——8
1 being the lowest and 8 being the highest.

WHAT ARE YOU SEEING?

Envy and cynicism are also predominant feelings. Many of these performers experience distrust. Some even believe that others will do them harm and that they must be on guard at all times, always alert, thinking about being upstaged onstage and off. And greed is evident in many whose self-centered attitudes lead them to demand more and more and more. The toxicity of *the diva syndrome* fight pattern often leaves the Pugnacious Performer alone with less and less and less. Their success is simply not sustainable because others experience their power and force as intimidating and overbearing, and ultimately refuse to work with them.

The diva syndrome's outcome-focused patterns are also vividly manifest in Pugnacious Performers as their desired outcome is to *win*, at any and all cost. They will seemingly defend the results they want to the death. They boss others around with threats and a self-righteous attitude.

REFLECTION 60

How much do you need to win?

1——2——3——4——5——6——7——8
1 being the lowest and 8 being the highest.

WHAT ARE YOU SEEING?

Performers who show up with overpowering dissonant energy are often associated with the offstage designation of drama queen: false persona, fake tears, lies, exaggerated or fabricated illnesses, imaginary scenarios—drama to manipulate situations and others to get their desired results. Their ruthless ambition drives most of their interactions. The mantra of a Pugnacious Performer is, "I want what I want when I want it."

REFLECTION 61

How often have you been called a drama queen?

1——2——3——4——5——6——7——8

1 being the lowest and 8 being the highest.

WHAT ARE YOU SEEING?

Pugnacious Performers do stand up for themselves—by *standing and stomping on everyone else*. They are most definitely problem-focused; but the problem is *everyone and everything else* in their lives.

They are self-absorbed, high-maintenance, judgmental, entitled, and defensive; and they blame the world for anything that doesn't go their way. They are consumed by and fixated on who and what is to blame when things don't go as planned.

These are quotes I've heard in my office:

> "It's his fault—if he had set the alarm, I would've been on time for rehearsal."

> "They ought to cart that conductor away."

> "Had they brought in a better choreographer, I would have performed much better."

> "Get out of my way."

> "Had I been born with those opportunities, I'd be getting those roles."

> "How can she be so stupid?"

> "I'm glad she left, I didn't love her anyway."

> "He screwed his way to the top."

> "I'll just step on his lines."

> "What do the critics know?"

Incapacitated by their dissonant energy, Pugnacious Performers are unable to think in shades of gray. They think in binary ways: right or wrong, good or bad, *It's my way or the highway.* Their way is the only way.

REFLECTION 62

How much do you need to be right?

1——2——3——4——5——6——7——8

1 being the lowest and 8 being the highest.

WHAT ARE YOU SEEING?

Their rigidity is rooted in judgment—a subjective belief. Pugnacious Performers cling to their judgments as a kind of security blanket that seems necessary for their self-respect and self-esteem.

REFLECTION 63

How judgmental are you?

1——2——3——4——5——6——7——8

1 being the lowest and 8 being the highest.

WHAT ARE YOU SEEING?

Pugnacious Performers' inflexibility leaves them powerless to conceive of possibilities and opportunities, other than what satisfies them. Possibility represents a threat to their point of view. Anyone who seems to disagree is considered to be disloyal, as Pugnacious Performers take it personally. The definition of possibility is very specific to the Pugnacious Performer. They are suspicious of whatever is different from the way they think and what they want. Possibility is therefore a negative: anything other than what is in their head and heart is perceived as a threat to their control, their power, their identity, and their being.

Write your definition of possibility:

The diva syndrome's pattern of taking things personally is glaringly conspicuous as Pugnacious Performers simply assume that everything is always ALL ABOUT ME! They are self-absorbed and self-centered; they are unable to walk in another's shoes and their oft-time abundant charisma covers up a dissonant-filled lack of empathy.

They go around with their hurt feelings, all the time believing that their feelings define reality. They find hurt in any situation, statement, or facial expression. There's rarely a time when a Pugnacious Performer's feelings are not hurt. However, the reality is that their gross insensitivity hurts the feelings of others.

REFLECTION 64

How often are your feelings hurt?

1——2——3——4——5——6——7——8
1 being the lowest and 8 being the highest.

WHAT ARE YOU SEEING?

Pugnacious Performers use their eerie interpretive powers to manipulate the Achilles' heels of others. They know where others are vulnerable and use it to their advantage, often to elicit retribution and revenge.

When someone needs center stage all the time and feels deprived of it, the effect on everyone else is predictably destructive. Those in their midst either give them the spotlight, walk on eggshells, or walk away wounded.

REFLECTION 65

How much do you need to be center stage?

1——2——3——4——5——6——7——8
1 being the lowest and 8 being the highest.

WHAT ARE YOU SEEING?

Although *the diva syndrome* patterns are intertwined, it's important to understand each one of them separately to appreciate how some performers reach their performance potential and how many others do not.

The overpowering dissonant energy in the personalities of the Problem-Ridden and Pugnacious Performers not only embodies *the diva syndrome*; it also prevents harmonic energy from developing, thus preventing these artists from even thinking about the performance potential they have inside.

As you leave the first two profiles and move on to the next, I would like to offer a reflection which you might consider practicing daily.

REFLECTION 66

How much dissonant energy did you experience and express today?

1——2——3——4——5——6——7——8
1 being the lowest and 8 being the highest.

WHAT ARE YOU SEEING?

Of course, everyone experiences and expresses dissonant energy and each of *the diva syndrome* patterns. Everyone expresses flight-or-fight energy when overwhelmed and unable to see other options. Everyone focuses on results and outcomes, taking themselves out of the performance moment. Everyone fails to see possibilities when clinging to the familiar and their need to be right. And everyone interprets the world personally in moments of tunnel-vision and self-absorption.

In the first two profiles you were offered 18 Reflections.

**Take note and count the number of
1's, 2's, 3's, and 4's that you've recorded.**

**How many of these low numbers
did you record in your responses?**

In my work, I have concluded that any number below 5 indicates that you are not suffering *the diva syndrome* and do not fit the profile of either The Problem-Ridden or Pugnacious Performer. *You are on the ascent!*

Yet, you may see yourself reflected in the personality of the Problem-Ridden or Pugnacious Performer, and experience and express dissonant energy and *diva syndrome* patterns more regularly. However, you can learn to shift from primarily dissonant to primarily harmonic energy and learn how to reach your performance potential. In the next profile, you will learn how.

THE PROMISING PERFORMER
PERSONALITY PROFILE

The third performer personality profile is transitional. Promising Performers are shifting from dissonant to harmonic energy, moving beyond *the diva syndrome*, which enables them to function well and experience success, both onstage and off. Promising Performers are on the rise. They are moving forward in their lives with congenial, cooperative, and generous ways of showing up. Although their performance potential is not fully realized, these performers are taking responsibility and are accountable for their thoughts, feelings, personality characteristics, and behaviors.

Yet, Promising Performers come to my office knowing that they have more inside.

Quotes that I have heard include:

"I have more to express."

"I know I am successful but there's got to be more."

"I am stuck."

"Stuck" is the Promising Performer's refrain. What prevents them from realizing their performance potential?

Promising Performers don't yet have a firm sense of identity. Honoring wants and needs is essential in the formation of self. However, these performers neglect, overlook, dismiss—and many are even unaware of—their needs and wants, which prevents them from reaching their performance potential.

REFLECTION 67

How much or often do you honor your wants and needs?

1——2——3——4——5——6——7——8
1 being the lowest and 8 being the highest.

WHAT ARE YOU SEEING?

Promising Performers discount their own wants and needs by rationalizing and behaving altruistically, which ironically can be self-serving as they continue to be self-absorbed. Unlike the Problem-Ridden Performer whose solution to a problem is flight, and the Pugnacious Performer, whose solution is fight, Promising Performers are motivated by a need to find peace of mind. Everyone wants to find peace of mind. However, Promising Performers want to feel better even if it means putting their performance potential in jeopardy. They focus on the problems of others, seeming to place the wants and needs of others first. They seek relief from conflict and chaos by avoiding confrontation, disagreement, and rocking the boat. They make choices to bring about recovery and equilibrium—comfort-driven choices.

It's still "All about me," as, by taking care of you I'm taking care of me. This is accomplished through rationalization and altruistic ways of being and behaving without having to acknowledge wants and needs.

Rationalization is characterized by assigning thoughts and feelings to causes that can seem reasonable and valid but, in truth, are unrelated to facts.

Rationalization can be a wonderful way to get on with your life as it can take you out of the despair and darkness of the first two profiles and walk you into the sunlight. Yet, it can also keep you walking on eggshells. Rationalization can be uncomfortable because it doesn't leave space for self-care. It causes you to do things that you might not really believe in and doesn't always allow your true values to shine. Although it can feel like a breath of fresh air, the air is at times a bit stale and choky. It's a balancing act.

How does rationalization show up in your life?

Promising Performers are masters at rationalization: at justifying, explaining, numbing, excusing, and pleasing.

REFLECTION 68

How much do you justify?

1——2——3——4——5——6——7——8
1 being the lowest and 8 being the highest.

WHAT ARE YOU SEEING?

How much do you explain?

1——2——3——4——5——6——7——8

1 being the lowest and 8 being the highest.

WHAT ARE YOU SEEING?

How much do you numb yourself?

1——2——3——4——5——6——7——8

1 being the lowest and 8 being the highest.

WHAT ARE YOU SEEING?

What is your numbing agent of choice?

WHAT ARE YOU SEEING?

How often do you make excuses?

1——2——3——4——5——6——7——8

1 being the lowest and 8 being the highest.

WHAT ARE YOU SEEING?

How much do you strive to please others?

1——2——3——4——5——6——7——8

1 being the lowest and 8 being the highest.

WHAT ARE YOU SEEING?

In order to rationalize, Promising Performers also reframe. Reframing is the ability to outline or express an idea, thought or concept in different terms, which can be a way to see more "positive" alternatives — or, another way to *serve* the framer's self-denial of his or her own wants and needs.

Quotes heard in my office from performers who identify with this profile include:

"I don't want to make waves."

"There's always a silver lining."

"My need has nothing to do with this."

"I don't care."

"I can make lemonade out of lemons."

"Everything will work out OK."

"That would be selfish."

"What I want is not relevant."

"It's better than nothing."

"I'll just be compliant."

"I'll just make do."

"It's fine."

"I make him happy."

"I can do it myself."

Promising Performers settle, compromise, tolerate, and forgive to feel better. They tolerate resentments and disappointments to gain peace of mind. These performers cooperate in order to find relief and calm.

REFLECTION 69

How much are you tolerating?

1——2——3——4——5——6——7——8

1 being the lowest and 8 being the highest.

WHAT ARE YOU SEEING?

REFLECTION 70

How much are you settling?

1——2——3——4——5——6——7——8

1 being the lowest and 8 being the highest.

WHAT ARE YOU SEEING?

REFLECTION 71

How much do you compromise?

1——2——3——4——5——6——7——8

1 being the lowest and 8 being the highest.

WHAT ARE YOU SEEING?

All these acts—particularly forgiving—clear away dissonant energy making space for more harmonic energy, as performers release bad experiences and choose good ones.

Forgiving is essentially for the forgiver, however, and therefore it is self-serving. Think of someone whom you cannot or will not forgive.

REFLECTION 72

*How much will your forgiveness release
your dissonant energy, making space
for your harmonic energy?*

1——2——3——4——5——6——7——8

1 being the lowest and 8 being the highest.

WHAT ARE YOU SEEING?

TABLEAU FIFTEEN: SAMUEL

A performer I'll call Samuel came into therapy feeling stuck in his music. He told me: "I've wanted to be principal cellist for years. My colleagues don't respect me. I'm just not good enough."

"Sam, what does I'm not good enough mean to you?" I asked.

Like many performers, Sam responded, "Well, I'm not perfect."

"And how would it be possible to be perfect?"

Performers want a magic pill to achieve perfection. It has to be magic, because how possible is perfection?

"How many hours do you practice daily?" I asked.

Instead of answering the question, Samuel began giving me reasons why he couldn't practice. They ranged from feeding his dog, working on his chimney–which had turned into a six-year project—lunching with friends, shopping, attending to a sick aunt, and finishing a needlepoint project to cover his piano bench.

"You see, I just can't get to my fiddle," he explained.

After Sam's extensive list of what felt to me like rationalizations, I asked him, "How else do you fiddle around?"

Sam said, "Well, I do have an occasional drink."

Yes, indeed, Sam had been having his occasional drink for more than twenty years.

He was afraid he was "not good enough," and used rationalizations to keep him from working. He was afraid to test the sustainability of his significant, natural musical talent and abilities through practice, learning new repertoire, listening to music, and playing with other musicians. He made fear-based decisions to distract himself with his aunt, his chimney, shopping, and by numbing himself. Alcohol was his main numbing agent. His rationalizations for why he didn't have enough time fed and enabled his fear-based choices.

Before we could move forward with the "good enough" therapy work, Sam wrestled with Mr. A, as he referred to his occasional drink. Sam eventually joined AA and began to work the program. I was then able to suggest that Sam consider a formula for excellence I had developed, which he started practicing.

Sam would bring his cello to therapy and started playing on my office stage. We also made contracts about how much he would practice daily. Once Sam started, his fingers loosened, and he heard his sound again; he began to like practicing and the music he was making. He remembered why he had chosen music.

I'm not good enough thinking is always related to doing or NOT doing the work. The rationalizations are always self-serving. For Sam, his rationalizations were ways to avoid doing the work that would prove to him if he were good enough.

Three and a half sober years later, Sam became principal in his orchestra and he began to play chamber music in a quartet with his colleagues. "I'm getting good enough now," he told me.

What does good enough mean to you?

Practice your own Good Enough Formula to achieve *excellence*.

1. Current hours of daily practice:
   Desired hours of daily practice:
   How can I make this happen?

2. Current hours devoted to learning new repertoire daily:
   Desired hours to be devoted to learning new repertoire daily:
   How can I make this happen?

3. Current hours devoted to listening daily
       (observing others in the field):
   Desired hours to be devoted to listening daily
       (observing others in the field):
   How can I make this happen?

4. Current hours playing with others daily:
   Desired hours playing with others daily:
   How can I make this happen?

Although rationalization is subjective and self-involved, it *is* a creative, imaginative talent and gift, and therefore harmonic. Promising Performers' harmonic energy will carry these performers forward into their performance lives powerfully. The more creative you are at rationalizing in the service of stretching and moving forward, the more empowered you will be.

Performers who show up as Promising Performers are also masters at altruistic ways of being and behaving. Altruistic thinking and behaving are characterized by rescuing or fixing others. In reality, they can also be self-serving. It's still all about me, under the guise of *it's all about you...*

However, everyone is aware that with altruistic ways of being and behaving, there are remarkable personal and professional benefits.

Promising Performers speak endlessly about how truly accomplished they feel when helping others through their consideration, comfort, caring, and compassion. Their significant harmonic energy is evident through their concern for others, which is enormously beneficial for ensemble, orchestral, corps work, and other work environments. They are often rewarded for their selflessness as their focus on others can lead to happiness and success as they foster teamwork and loyalty. Promising Performers are grateful for their gifts and in turn give generously and abundantly to their colleagues as well as to their audiences. They take very little personally and give without judgment. They inspire those around them and help bring out the performance potential of others. Promising Performers receive enormous accolades for their contributions.

REFLECTION 73

How much positive recognition do you receive for your giving?

1——2——3——4——5——6——7——8
1 being the lowest and 8 being the highest.

WHAT ARE YOU SEEING?

However, altruism—sacrificing in the service of others—may cause their own performances to suffer. Being of service to others *can* supersede their need to take care of themselves. These performers often neglect themselves, thinking that others' needs are more important than theirs. For example, many abandon their practice and rehearsal time to help colleagues, and many put their financial security at risk, thereby undermining their own work and performance potential.

REFLECTION 74

How often do the needs of others supersede your own needs?

1——2——3——4——5——6——7——8
1 being the lowest and 8 being the highest.

WHAT ARE YOU SEEING?

Here are other quotes heard in my office from Promising Performers:

"I want to play the pieces that they like—and that makes me as happy as playing my own compositions."

"I should've gone to the doctor, but she asked me to help her."

"I can't accept that."

"My chamber group comes before my cello concert."

"He needed the money more than I did."

"I gave up my spot center stage."

"I did all this and yet no one appreciates me."

Altruistic ways of being and behaving also involve challenges with taking. Everyone has a different comfort level when accepting compliments, gifts, praise, help, and even love.

REFLECTION 75

How comfortable are you with taking?

1——2——3——4——5——6——7——8
1 being the lowest and 8 being the highest.

WHAT ARE YOU SEEING?

In my work with Promising Performers, I have found that taking feels like a weakness to many of them. Their inability to *take* stems from the fact that they find their worthiness and self-esteem in giving, be it self-serving or not. Their discomfort with taking is especially evident when it comes to applause, particularly when taking their bows or curtain calls—whether on the formal stage or the stage of life.

REFLECTION 76

Stand in front of a mirror.
Close your eyes and imagine that you have performed
well and praise is about to be given to you.
Take a bow in front of the mirror.

Scale your comfort when receiving acclaim.

1——2——3——4——5——6——7——8
1 being the lowest and 8 being the highest.

WHAT ARE YOU SEEING?

If you scaled under 5, what were your thoughts
and feelings about receiving appreciation?

How do your thoughts and feelings about being given
thanks impact your performance potential?

WHAT ARE YOU SEEING?

The problems of others drive Promising Performers because they find their self-worth in helping and fixing. They get caught up in anyone's and everyone's drama.

Promising Performers sympathize with others, feel sorry for them, often see others as damaged, and are driven to fix them. They are determined to be the hero. Yet when the people whom they have helped no longer need them, these performers feel slighted and may shift all the way back to the dissonant behaviors in the Problem-Ridden Performer personality. They have sacrificed their own professional opportunities and futures to the extent that they are perceived as martyrs. They feel victimized. In addition, their intention to be of service can be more about being liked than being productive.

REFLECTION 77

How often do you feel taken advantage of or unappreciated?

1——2——3——4——5——6——7——8
1 being the lowest and 8 being the highest.

WHAT ARE YOU SEEING?

To enable (v.): to give power or means to; to make possible or easy.

Promising Performers are expert enablers. Enabling can be crippling to the very people they purport to help. Some pit musicians bring drugs to colleagues who struggle with addiction in the name of friendship. Helping another persist in a behavior that is self-destructive benefits the enabler. I worked with a performer who manipulated an environment for a showmance, which made her feel indispensable. Another lied to seemingly protect an artist who committed sexually abuse in order to "keep the peace" and to make himself feel important. These are harsh examples. However, enabling is one of the most dissonant and self-serving dimensions of altruism.

REFLECTION 78

How much do your altruistic ways of being and behaving impact your performance potential?

1——2——3——4——5——6——7——8

1 being the lowest and 8 being the highest.

WHAT ARE YOU SEEING?

TABLEAU SIXTEEN: NED

Ned was a stage actor who always received rave reviews not only for his acting prowess but also for stepping in as an understudy and saving the day. He was the eldest of five children, three brothers and one sister. When each sibling arrived, Ned did much of the mothering, as his father had died and his mother was overwhelmed. Therefore, when he was young, he was never known for who he was, but for what he did: filling in. Even as a child offstage, Ned was the "understudy."

As an adult, as he progressed in his profession, he became known in the business as a quick learner and an amazing, versatile performer. In New York and around the country he was called upon over the years to cover many roles. Ned made himself indispensable and received acknowledgment for "helping out"—rescuing—and he began to think of himself as a fixer, a kind of hero. That's where he got his recognition.

However, in his adult family life, he became aware that he was once again the understudy, as his wife favored her family of origin over him and their child, and he became rageful toward his wife. "I don't want to be second."

Ned was a Promising Performer whose altruistic ways of being and behaving were no longer serving him and were preventing him from reaching his performance potential. When he came into therapy, I introduced him to a tool that I developed, the Drama/Trauma Triangle.

The Drama Trauma Triangle

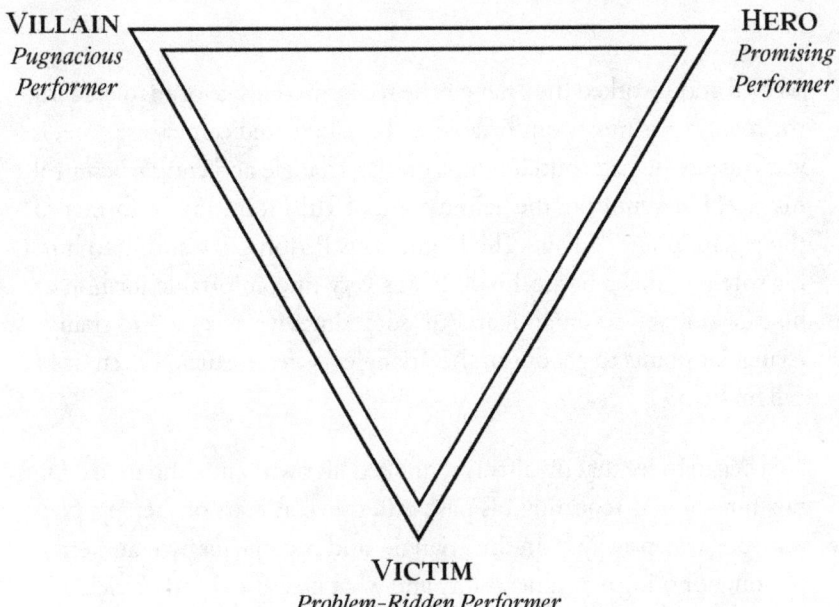

VILLAIN
Pugnacious Performer

HERO
Promising Performer

VICTIM
Problem-Ridden Performer

The Drama/Trauma Triangle describes three archetypal roles: Hero, Villain, and Victim. Each role corresponds with one of three Performer Personality Profiles: The Problem-Ridden Performer—Victim; The Pugnacious Performer—Villain; and The Promising Performer—Hero.

The Villain (Pugnacious Performer) sits at the upper left corner of the equilateral Triangle. The Villain is a persecutor; someone who intentionally bullies, hurts, humiliates, and blames others and is full of rage. At the bottom point of the Triangle is the Victim (Problem-Ridden Performer), full of fear, apathy, hopelessness, and hurt. At the upper right corner of the Triangle is the Hero (Promising Performer), the fixer, rescuer, helper, and enabler. The Hero is full of pity and sympathy.

These roles, however, are not static; they change situation by situation. Although you have a favorite role, you will note that you also "run around the triangle," playing the other two roles. The Drama/Trauma Triangle is a tool to help you visualize yourself running around the triangle, stuck in roles that keep you from reaching your performance potential.

The goal of this tool is to leave the Triangle, by withdrawing from the roles of Hero/Villain/Victim. When you retire these archetypal roles, you learn to play the role of a lifetime, your authentic self.

As Ned and I worked the Triangle, he recognized his favorite role, Hero, the role he was most comfortable with. When Ned came to see me, it was because he had shifted points on the Triangle and couldn't control his rage. He went from the heroic point of The Promising Performer to the rageful point, Villain, The Pugnacious Performer, wanting to hurt his wife and make her feel bad. It was very uncomfortable for him as his new role was so unfamiliar. But, sometimes it's necessary to change triangular points to get out of the Triangle, to get unstuck. Often, it's a call for help.

Ned began to see that his altruism masked his own wants and needs. He saw how he was repeating his past. After several years of therapy, Ned was able to step away from the Triangle, and become his own authentic person, honoring his vulnerability and what he wanted and needed. He divorced his wife, bought a New York apartment, started film and TV work, and told his agent he would understudy no more. He became a star in his own right. Ned made his claim and took center stage!

When Ned stepped away from the Triangle, he became a resplendent Potential-Realized Performer, strong enough to admit his wants, needs and vulnerabilities. Only then could he achieve what he was capable of—his performance potential.

REFLECTION 79

What is your favorite role on the Triangle?

How much time do you spend performing this role?

1——2——3——4——5——6——7——8
1 being the lowest and 8 being the highest.

WHAT ARE YOU SEEING?

What triggers a role change for you?

How often do you change roles?

1——2——3——4——5——6——7——8
1 being the lowest and 8 being the highest.

WHAT ARE YOU SEEING?

*How much does the Triangle interfere with
your performance potential?*

1——2——3——4——5——6——7——8
1 being the lowest and 8 being the highest.

WHAT ARE YOU SEEING?

Promising Performers have more harmonic energy than dissonant. However, they are still stretching, not fully reaping the rewards of fulfilling all that they can be. Yet, at this level of harmonic energy, Promising Performers enjoy a good life! And it is often at this point that these artists and I part company.

Over the years, the Problem-Ridden, Pugnacious and Promising Performers with whom I worked helped me see what was preventing performers on all the stages of their lives from reaching that possibility they have inside, and, at the same time, what empowers them to realize their full potential.

THE POTENTIAL-REALIZED PERFORMER PERSONALITY PROFILE

Potential-Realized Performers experience:

"that promise,"

"that stretch,"

"that reach,"

"that living up to"

"that special greatness,"

"a uniqueness"

"that possibility that they have inside,"

"something that perhaps they had never even dared to say aloud."

"…becoming the best they can be as people and as performers."

They practice harmonic energy at its crescendo, with great eye contact, a memorable and contagious smile, and laughing eyes. Their self-care and self-respect are apparent. These performers have a strong sense of self, based on a conscious awareness of who they are. They are aligned with what they do and how they do it.

Potential-Realized Performers tune into their harmonic energy at such a special intensity that I came to call it Performance Energy.

PERFORMANCE ENERGY

**Performance Energy is the
foundation of performance potential.**

Performance Energy is that IT factor; that *je ne sais quoi* energy; the energy that leaves the audience—whoever your audience is—screaming for more. It's the energy of change, of trust, the energy that says, "I am your person." It's that "I want what he's got" energy. It's contagious, electric, and charismatic.

Performance Energy is the energy of inspiration and that of memorable divas. It's the energy of those you want to be near, whose success you want to be part of. Performance Energy is the energy that subtly changes audiences inside and out. It empowers performers to rise to divine pinnacles and reach performance potential. Performance Energy is the energy of greatness, when you are motivated and excited to see the possibilities available to you and everyone else.

Potential-Realized Performers also choose identifiable, specific thoughts, feelings, characteristics, and behaviors that support and sustain them in realizing their special performance uniqueness. They show up, onstage and off, in ways that energize them to realize their performance potential.

A major difference that I noted about Potential-Realized Performers was *how* they think. Many Potential-Realized Performers embrace a mantra that I live by, and I encourage you too to embrace it wholeheartedly.

> *"When you change what you're thinkin',
> you will change what you're doin'…"*

Therefore, please get up on your feet as I find it's much more powerful to experience while standing. So, on your toes and say it out loud. On the beat:

> *"When you change what you're thinkin',
> you will change what you're doin'…"*

When you change your thoughts, you work through *the diva syndrome*, you become unstuck, you change what you do, you change your behavior, you change your performance.

THOUGHTS: A REPERTOIRE OF FOUR
EMPOWERING WAYS OF THINKING

Powered by Performance Energy, Potential-Realized Performers practice four ways of thinking that make reaching their performance potential look easy:

- Process-focused thinking

- Possibility-driven thinking

- Judgment-free thinking

- Depersonalized thinking

If these ways of thinking are not already a part of your thoughtful repertoire, adopting them will change your life.

Practicing them can help if you suffer from *the diva syndrome*, if you are *stuck*, and when your thoughts are preventing you from reaching your performance potential. These ways of thinking are mindsets, how you *set your mind*, how you think about how you perform onstage and off.

Process-Focused Thinking

What does performance mean to you?

Consider that any time you approach your work YOU ARE IN PER-FORMANCE. You are performing… in the practice room, in auditions, in rehearsals, in lessons, and, of course, what is traditionally referred to as "the performance." You are thinking about your performances much of the time. Aren't your thoughts about performance, then, some of your most powerful?

There are two ways of thinking about performance: One prevents you from reaching your performance potential, the other empowers it.

If you're thinking about the *results* of your performance, while performing, and how it will end, you're thinking performance- defeating thoughts.

If you're thinking about what you are doing in the moment of performance, you are thinking empowering, energizing thoughts.

Being Outcome-Focused

This approach to performance is the outcome way of thinking or mindset and is part of *the diva syndrome.* Outcome thinking focuses on results, on what's *going* to happen. Outcome-focused thoughts are *not* performance-enhancing.

Outcome-focused thoughts that I have heard in my office include:

"Will I be brilliant?"

"Will I make the same mistake?"

"Am I impressing my agent?"

"Am I going to be successful?"

"What will go wrong?"

"How do I look?"

"Can I hit that note?"

"Will I go up on my lines?"

"It's all about me!"

"This performance means everything to my career."

REFLECTION 80

How much do you think about the results of what you are doing while you are doing it?

1——2——3——4——5——6——7——8
1 being the lowest and 8 being the highest.

WHAT ARE YOU SEEING?

Outcome-Focused Questions

1. In what ONE area of your work life are you currently struggling with outcome-focused thinking?

2. How would your work life be different if you weren't focused on outcome and results?

3. In what ONE area of your personal life are you currently struggling with outcome-focused thinking?

4. How would your personal life be different if you weren't focused on outcome and results?

Outcomes are necessary. We all need to think about the kind of results we want before we can let them go — by adapting Process-Focused thinking, staying in the moment, staying in the hour, staying in the day — the only way to realize those results and outcome.

The second way to approach performance is Process-Focused thinking.

Being Process-Focused

1. Focus on where you are NOW, not where you want to be.

REFLECTION 81

How much are you in the now of your performance experiences?

1——2——3——4——5——6——7——8
1 being the lowest and 8 being the highest.

WHAT ARE YOU SEEING?

2. Focus on the progression of performing. Moving forward, step by step, moment to moment thinking is the way to achieve *anything*.

3. Focus on trusting and being with yourself. Your feelings and your intuition are valuable resources. Trust that you know your technique, so whatever happens, you are able to transcend it with elegance and grace. Your trust will yield extraordinary stamina and remarkable resilience. You will be so deeply rooted in the process that the unwelcome and the unexpected become creative opportunities.

A singer described it as, "A sense of abandonment, I go into a bubble, a zone, a flow..."

REFLECTION 82

When performing, how much do you trust yourself?

1——2——3——4——5——6——7——8

1 being the lowest and 8 being the highest.

WHAT ARE YOU SEEING?

---

4. Focus on knowing the difference between what is under your control and what is not.

Potential-Realized Performers derive their process-focused thinking from a high level of conscious awareness. Their awareness empowers them to concentrate on what is realistically and artistically manageable. Their long-term goals are motivated by feelings of pleasure and joy rather than by short-term happiness as the result of situational accomplishments and applause. Passion, connection, commitment and excellence are the life-long outcomes of process-focused thinking.

REFLECTION 83

*How much do you know the difference between
what is under your control and what is not?*

1——2——3——4——5——6——7——8
1 being the lowest and 8 being the highest.

WHAT ARE YOU SEEING?

With process-focused thinking, you continually learn and grow in performance and as a person.

TABLEAU SEVENTEEN: SIDNEY

"I can't get anything right." Sidney, a baritone, was on the cusp of a successful operatic career. *On the cusp* because he couldn't memorize his lines and was unfocused onstage. The prompter was always yelling at him. "Getting it right," extended into his personal life as well, particularly his intimate relationships. Sidney came into therapy because he believed he had problems with two techniques, vocal, and lovemaking. He thought that he was a failure at both.

"I'm so worried. I never hit this note." "I always miss that passage." "I never got along with that conductor." "He never likes the way I stroke his back." "What if he doesn't like the way I kiss him?" "I'm afraid that they'll fire me if I can't remember these lines." "What if he breaks up with me?" "I just can't get anything right."

We could have assigned Sidney's "not getting it right" to his ADHD; it would've been a logical and convenient explanation. In fact, he was given medication. However, Sidney's anxiety, his anguish and his inability to hold eye contact with me took us in a different direction.

"What does getting it right mean to you?" I inquired.

"Well, obviously, "Sidney responded, "It means that I'm just not enough."

As we began to understand what "not getting it right" meant to Sidney, we began to understand his on and offstage behaviors. The therapy was really about Sidney's self-esteem. His thoughts and feelings about himself were too negative for him to remain with himself. He was self-loathing; he simply could not stand himself. He could not be alone with his thoughts or his feelings, which meant he could not perform in the moment—so imperative in both lovemaking and performing on the stage: being with his music, with the text, with his colleagues and with his lovers. He fled into outcome thinking, worrying about the past and anxious about the future.

During Sidney's therapy, he learned to stay in the moment by sharing his negative thoughts and feelings with me in the therapy room. We used the stage in my office where he practiced performing in the moment—in the now—and we used our interaction and Sydney's feelings and thoughts about himself to allow him to be present. All his senses became alive. If he could do it in the therapy room with me, he could do it in the world, on the stage and in the bedroom. Because I always believe that how you perform one thing is how you perform everything.

For me, it was a very exciting therapy, as Sidney adopted process-focused thinking right before my eyes—in the moment—as he learned to like himself and learned to be with himself. We even laugh as he tells me there is no "right"—there is just *now*. He also tells me that the prompter now smiles when he's onstage.

What does process mean to you?

I think the late Stephen Sondheim says it best in *Sunday in the Park with George.*

"Bit by bit,
Putting it together...
Piece by piece"

A Broadway singer explained process to me, "...as being in the moment of what I was singing; I was in my performance experience."

A percussionist told me, "Process is a sensory experience. All my senses are alive, involved and active. They keep me present."

A dancer explained, "Process is a series of movements and steps performed as a way to achieve a particular end."

And a cellist said, "Process energizes me to be the best that I can be in each instant of performance."

An actor wept that process is, "just about *being.*"

Process-focused thinking is:

being in the performance moment... in the now

being in charge of what you can be in charge of—doing the work, being prepared

being... without worry or anxiety

being invested in what you're doing...

trusting yourself as the primary resource in your performance

With process-focused thinking, everyone is open to an inspired state of discovery, leading to moments of wonder and awe.

Potential-Realized Performers have their vision and stay in the moment, stay in the day. They are present. They live in their performance experience as they tap into their Performance Energy and use it to create ground-breaking work... awe-inspiring, jaw-dropping, gasping performance moments, onstage and off.

Potential-Realized Performers are so in the now that they are able to create something from nothing. They think and respond on their feet. Their belief that all that happens has value and purpose allows their sensory abilities to be unlimited. These performers are in charge of their performance life and choose their performance experiences. When you perform with a process-focused way of thinking, you will continually grow and improve.

While at Tanglewood, the esteemed summer music festival, in 1985, I witnessed fourteen-year-old world-class virtuoso violinist Midori perform the 5th movement of Bernstein's Serenade. She accidentally broke her E string and quickly passed her fiddle to the concertmaster who in turn gave her his. But then she again broke the E string on his instrument and she rapidly took the violin of the associate concertmaster, without missing a beat. You could literally have heard a pin drop. This is the epitome of being in the moment.

Possibility — Driven Thinking

Holding Hamlet's mirror, you'll now be able to recognize that when you're playing the violin and focusing on your mistakes, when you're memorizing a monologue and all you hear are the problems of the language, when you're at the barre and feeling the obstacles of your stiff joints, or when you awake with a stress headache, you are preventing yourself from reaching your performance potential.

Why?

Because you're focusing on the negative: what's wrong, problems, mistakes, obstacles.

REFLECTION 84

How often do you wake up in the morning thinking negative thoughts?

1——2——3——4——5——6——7——8
1 being the lowest and 8 being the highest.

WHAT ARE YOU SEEING?

If you answered 5 or above, it makes sense that you scaled high. Don't most of you look at things that way, having been weaned on "What's wrong?" and "What's the matter?" Haven't you been conditioned to think that everything has to do with problems? Even when things are right, what does everyone say? They say...*No problem!*

*How would you show up if you weren't
thinking about problems?*

After thirty-five years of working with members of the performing arts community, I have learned that focusing on problems, obstacles, mistakes and stress *doesn't work* to move you forward to reach your performance potential.

Problems, obstacles, mistakes, and stress keep you worrying about your past, second-guessing, focused on poor me, apologizing, complaining, blaming, and criticizing.

Potential -Realized Performers became empowered by changing their perspective and thinking possibility-driven thoughts.

*Remember... "When you change what you're thinkin',
you will change what you're doin'..."*

Possibility-Driven thinking is the art of seeing obstacles as opportunities, problems as possibilities, and mistakes as *learning*.

How about thinking that there really are no problems, there are no obstacles, no mistakes, no *stress*, even when the unexpected and unwelcome show up?

Think about stress...

What are your thoughts about stress?

REFLECTION 85

How much stress do you want in your life?

1——2——3——4——5——6——7——8
1 being the lowest and 8 being the highest.

WHAT ARE YOU SEEING?

If you scored 5 or below and you want to rid your life of stress, here's a new thought and perspective:

What if what you *really* want is for your *response* to stress to be different. Think of stress as an internal experience generated by your THOUGHTS because of something that is uncomfortable, unwelcome or unresolved in your life.

> **Stressor** (n.): a stimulus—an event, condition… The six traditional, identified stressors are: spiritual… ; they are often interrelated.

It is not only the performing arts that are filled with stressors which impact performance potential, everyone is susceptible and experiences one or more stressors much of the time. Only you are in charge of how you respond to them.

> *"When you change what you're thinkin',*
> *you will change what you're doin'…"*

…you will experience control over the six external stressors and you will behave differently. You can live a life of possibilities. Your performance will change.

Stressors

SPIRITUAL STRESSORS

Spiritual stressors cause you to question the meaning of life: your values, your purpose, your cultural norms and political beliefs, your goals, gifts or talents, and whether or not you are in alignment with them. Anyone may experience a crisis of values when they take on roles and tasks that devalue them, or feel pressured to make choices that don't align with their goals. Spiritual stress may also be triggered by joyless pursuits—sustained yet uninspired efforts toward the achievement of a meaningless purpose.

What are your spiritual stressors?

REFLECTION 86

How much do spiritual stressors impact your performance potential?

1——2——3——4——5——6——7——8

1 being the lowest and 8 being the highest.

WHAT ARE YOU SEEING?

Mental Stressors

When you are stretched too thin with too many demands; when your demands are too difficult or too easy; or when you lack focus and become distracted and preoccupied, you're mentally stressed. Anyone who is juggling a strict performance schedule while trying to be present for their family, exacerbated by financial pressures, may succumb to mental stress.

What are your mental stressors?

REFLECTION 87

How much do mental stressors impact your performance potential?

1——2——3——4——5——6——7——8

1 being the lowest and 8 being the highest.

WHAT ARE YOU SEEING?

EMOTIONAL STRESSORS

Emotional stressors occur when your needs and wants are not being met. When you don't even know what your needs and wants are! When you don't understand or can't figure out people or situations, when you don't know what you feel, or when you are unable to express the emotions that you do feel. When you're too busy taking care of the needs and wants of others…to name but a few!

What are your emotional stressors?

REFLECTION 88

How much do emotional stressors impact your performance potential?

1——2——3——4——5——6——7——8

1 being the lowest and 8 being the highest.

WHAT ARE YOU SEEING?

PHYSICAL STRESSORS

Everyone is confronted with physical stressors: when your bodies don't function optimally, when you don't get enough sleep, when you have weight issues, when you are injured, or ingest harmful chemicals or substances, such as alcohol and drugs. Given the rigorous demands of their art, dancers are especially subject to physical stressors as are vocal artists and actors whose very instruments are so precarious.

What are your physical stressors?

REFLECTION 89

How much do physical stressors impact your performance potential?

1——2——3——4——5——6——7——8
1 being the lowest and 8 being the highest.

WHAT ARE YOU SEEING?

ENVIRONMENTAL STRESSORS

Environmental stressors include inclement weather, noise, unwelcome odors, noxious chemicals, and hot and heavy costuming. They may also include a crowded or overheated stage or pit, or construction dust infecting your eyes and lungs. Sustained exposure to these irritations can greatly increase discomfort and aggression.

What are your environmental stressors?

REFLECTION 90

How much do environmental stressors impact your performance potential?

1——2——3——4——5——6——7——8
1 being the lowest and 8 being the highest.

WHAT ARE YOU SEEING?

SOCIAL STRESSORS

Last but not least, there are social conditions that cause stress. When other people are the problem: *"Oh, if only he, she, they, were different…"* When people don't behave in ways that you want or need them to. This might include verbal aggression from a colleague, friend, family member or any toxic group environment. Feelings are hurt, tempers heat up, and fears are stoked. Often over the blink of an eye or something imagined. Everyone is under pressure.

What are your social stressors?

REFLECTION 91

How much do social stressors impact your performance potential?

1——2——3——4——5——6——7——8
1 being the lowest and 8 being the highest.

WHAT ARE YOU SEEING?

Once you identify a stressor, you are able to change what you're thinking and choose how you want to respond. You are in control!

When you think about stress differently, a world of possibilities opens.

Now, let's think about mistakes.

TABLEAU EIGHTEEN:
THE YOUNG WOMAN, TAKE TWO

As a first-year student at The Neighborhood Playhouse, The Young Woman had the unique honor of being directed by Sir John Gielgud. During rehearsal, she proudly delivered her one line: "*The silver star.*"

Gielgud stopped the rehearsal and asked her to repeat her line. She eagerly did as he asked.

"Out!" he said. She looked at him questioningly. "Get out!" he repeated, "Where's your understudy?"

The Young Woman burst into tears. She had no idea what kind of horrible mistake she had made. "I disgraced myself in front of the other students; I've shamed The Neighborhood Playhouse and I won't be asked back for second year," she thought as she raced off the stage.

She later learned that Gielgud was reacting to her Midwestern accent. A fellow student told her, "He kicked you out because of your sibilant S."

Of course, it was understandable to be disappointed, but once she'd learned about her "horrible mistake," she could have turned it around and *thought* about it differently. What if the young woman had thought of the Gielgud situation as a learning experience?

She might have changed her thinking to, "Okay, I'm sad. Really upset. However, I see that in the long run he did me a favor. I'm going to speak to the school about studying diction. I will only get better at doing what I love."

Had the Young Woman thought differently about mistakes, she would have learned that when you accept that there are no mistakes, only learnings, you can discover new opportunities and focus on committing and connecting to what you love.

When was the last time you were performing and thought, "Oh, I just messed up—I made a mistake?"

REFLECTION 92

Think about a recent 'mistake' when working.

What happened?

What were you thinking?

WHAT ARE YOU SEEING?

My hope is that you no longer think, *"I made a mistake,"* but rather, *"I made a new learning."*

Potential-Realized Performers use 'mistakes' in their work and integrate them as new *learnings, growth, and development.*

What a relief…

REFLECTION 93

How often do you think and say can't, won't, shouldn't, don't ?

1——2——3——4——5——6——7——8
1 being the lowest and 8 being the highest.

WHAT ARE YOU SEEING?

Can'ts, shouldn'ts, couldn'ts, won'ts, and wouldn'ts make performance potential *impossible.*

However…

When you don't let what you cannot do interfere with what you can do, think of the possibilities.

You think positively

You move forward

The can'ts become *cans*
the don'ts… *dos*
the shouldn'ts… *shoulds*
the couldn'ts… *coulds*
the wont's… *wills*
the wouldn'ts… *woulds*…

The brain does not recognize the word 'not.' If you focus on what you don't want, nine times out of ten you get… *what you don't want.*

Potential-Realized Performers tell me that when they begin to think that so-called problems, mistakes, and obstacles are ways to reach their potential, they become genuinely as excited by the things that do *not* go as planned as by the things that do. They learn to love the unexpected. Their Performance Energy empowers them to think about the opportunities and possibilities when they go up on a line, slip onstage, break a string, the hall is too cold, they're late for a callback, lose an audition, crack on a note, close a show, Potential-Realized Performers think: Where's the opportunity here? What's possible?

Thoughts determine how you handle these situations. Thoughts shape how you perform.

How to make the impossible possible?

Possibility-driven Questions

1. In what ONE area of your work life do you currently see no possibilities?

2. How would you show up if you were thinking about this area as a possibility and an opportunity?

3. In what ONE area of your personal life do you currently see no possibilities?

4. How would you show up if you were thinking about this area as a possibility and an opportunity?

How to make the possible impossible?

Two performers—Radine and Gretchen—came into my office making *the possible impossible* in two ways: *assumptions and limiting beliefs*. These ways of thinking were blocking their Performance Energy and keeping them from becoming Potential-Realized Performers.

> **Assumption** (n.): something that is accepted as true or as certain to happen again, without proof.

TABLEAU NINETEEN: RADINE

Radine refused to take an audition because the casting director had seen her three times and had never cast her. She assumed that this time would be no different; he had not chosen her before, why would he choose her now? Radine made an *assumption* that winning the role that she had her heart set on would be impossible.

And indeed, Radine examined her assumption, thinking, *"Maybe I can make this audition different this time."* She took control, telling her agent she'd take the audition. She prepared for the audition differently, prepared her sides differently, went in with a different attitude. She did the work and won the role. She changed her thinking; she changed her attitude; she showed up differently and realized her performance potential.

REFLECTION 94

Think of an assumption that you've made in your work life.

How costly was that assumption?

1——2——3——4——5——6——7——8
1 being the lowest and 8 being the highest.

WHAT ARE YOU SEEING?

How to make the impossible possible?

If you think: *This is impossible.*
Ask yourself: How true is that?
Just because it happened once or ten times…
does that mean it will happen again?

When you change your perspective, you will change your behavior.

How to make the possible impossible?

Limiting belief (n.): a thought that is accepted without question as truth, learned from a person or an institution that is valued, loved, idealized, esteemed, treasured or venerated.

TABLEAU TWENTY: GRETCHEN

"I guess my mother was right. I should get a real job. I can't make money in musical theater." Gretchen was about to quit when she was cast in Mamma Mia. She had been temping for a year and a half, and had come so close to getting principal roles but her mother's words *"Get a real job"* seemed stronger than any praise, industry promise or therapy. She's doing very well now as a performer and all I can say is perhaps the universe stepped in. But the power of a limiting belief cannot be overestimated.

How to make the impossible possible?

How do you challenge a limiting belief?

When a thought is accepted without question as truth, acknowledge the importance and significance it has played in your life.

Understanding and working through a limiting belief is a slow process. On the one hand, a limiting belief has been very valuable, as it's provided structure and guidance. On the other hand, a limiting belief is just that… limiting, if not preventing, your performance potential.

In Gretchen's life, her mother was teaching her fiscal responsibility. However, Gretchen is an artist and was well aware that she was in a profession where financial stability was anything but normative. Gretchen was experiencing a value conflict.

Limiting beliefs are so difficult to face because they bring important, time-honored values into conflict. If Gretchen followed her dreams and became a full-time performer, she was afraid that she would lose her mother and become penniless. And if she did find a "real job," she was afraid she would lose herself.

REFLECTION 95

Think of a belief that you have in your work life, that you accept without question.

How much does that belief serve you now?

1——2——3——4——5——6——7——8

1 being the lowest and 8 being the highest.

WHAT ARE YOU SEEING?

Working through a limiting belief and the conflicting values that are at its foundation is a process that takes time, courage, reflection, contemplation and an acknowledgment that the truth that was so much a part of your thinking repertoire has lost its validity in your life today.

THE PRINCESS/PRINCE AND THE FROG

You may, at times, feel cursed or even under a spell. In your nightmares, or when things are just not going your way, you may feel stuck, trapped in a dark, dank underworld… you may even believe that you're a frog! You may have been told by somebody you dearly love that you're a slimy, green, wart-covered, eye-bulging, pond-dwelling creature—full of traits to which are assigned negative values and, therefore, unworthy of love and respect.

You may recognize your froghood as a limiting belief, and ask:
How true is that?

*"When you change what you're thinkin',
you will change what you're doin'…"*

Picture the frog turning into a princess/prince.

Imagine the frog seeing a throne instead of a lily pad, embracing her/his differences, celebrating the things that frogs do: jumping, croaking, projecting their slimy tongues and eating lizards; accepting who she/he is and what she/he does and by doing so loving herself/himself, winning roles, touching audiences. Directors, choreographers, work colleagues, family and friends can't help but embrace her/him as she/he emerges from the beautiful murky water as a princess/prince.

If you see yourself as a frog, think: Where's the opportunity to do something new, different, unique, and innovative? Where can I think creatively and curiously, out of the box?

The frogs in my office adopted a possibility-driven way of thinking, seeing obstacles as opportunities, mistakes as learnings, and problems as possibilities. Many also worked through their limiting beliefs.

These frogs began to croak differently, in ways that were creative and unique to them; they jumped to new heights, in ways that were pleasing because they were expressing themselves. They were so happy with their colors and their various shades that their princes and princesses emerged. They had royalty in them all along.

They made the impossible possible. These frogs became Potential-Realized Performers reaching their performance potential.

With possibility-driven thinking, dissonant energy, *the diva syndrome* and being stuck are no longer possible. You are in charge of your life, onstage and off. No stress! No obstacles! No mistakes! No problems! You now think about opportunities, learning, and possibilities. You are a Potential-Realized Performer.

Judgment-Free Thinking

TABLEAU TWENTY-ONE: SANDY

Sandy was one of the most sought-after horn players in the jazz world. He had such a glorious and recognizable sound. Everyone wanted to play with him but most avoided him socially. Sandy was so unpleasant. There was nothing he didn't criticize both musically and personally.

I knew who he was when he entered my office. I also knew his reputation and that I would be in for it. And indeed I was. He hated the Hirschfelds on my wall. He hated the fact that I wear mostly black. He hated that I play classical music in my waiting room. He hated my nasal twang and was constantly correcting my grammar. There was nothing that he wasn't judgmental about.

As much as Sandy could not say anything nice to anyone, he could not believe anything positive that was said about him either, both professionally and certainly not personally. Judgment was his only way of being in charge and feeling superior, immune from needing anyone. At one point he said, "I don't mean to insult you, but…" I replied, "Really?" And we were off.

Sandy's teacher never ever said a kind word about Sandy's music-making. Sandy started studying with him when he was nine years old. His teacher was his primary caregiver and mentor. "I worshipped him," he told me. Sandy moved from Utah into the home of a New York family where he lived until he graduated from a prominent conservatory. He and the family had little interaction.

Sandy eventually told me that had he shared his loneliness and his isolation with his teacher, his teacher would have considered him weak, and that his music should be the only thing that mattered in his life.

He came into therapy because he was having trouble with his embouchure. His mouth was beginning to twitch and there was no discernible medical reason for this trembling. Sandy was scared.

In many ways judgmental thinking is default thinking. Our culture is flooded with judgment. Many of us have painful memories of disapproving parents and other important childhood figures, critical remarks throughout formative school years, dismissive comments from so-called friends, and condemning observations at work. Judgmental thinking is rife with dissonant energy and is a sure way to prevent performance potential.

Everyone has their own judgmental-thinking style. The following Judgmental-Thinking Scales will help you acknowledge and understand yours. Awareness of the extent to which you are judgmental provides a venue for change.

REFLECTION 96

Judgmental-Thinking Scales

How often do you think that you are the smartest in the room?

1——2——3——4——5——6——7——8
1 being the lowest and 8 being the highest.

WHAT ARE YOU SEEING?

How often do you think in polarities:
good and bad, right and wrong, black and white?

1——2——3——4——5——6——7——8
1 being the lowest and 8 being the highest.

WHAT ARE YOU SEEING?

How often do you think that you should be in control?

1——2——3——4——5——6——7——8
1 being the lowest and 8 being the highest.

WHAT ARE YOU SEEING?

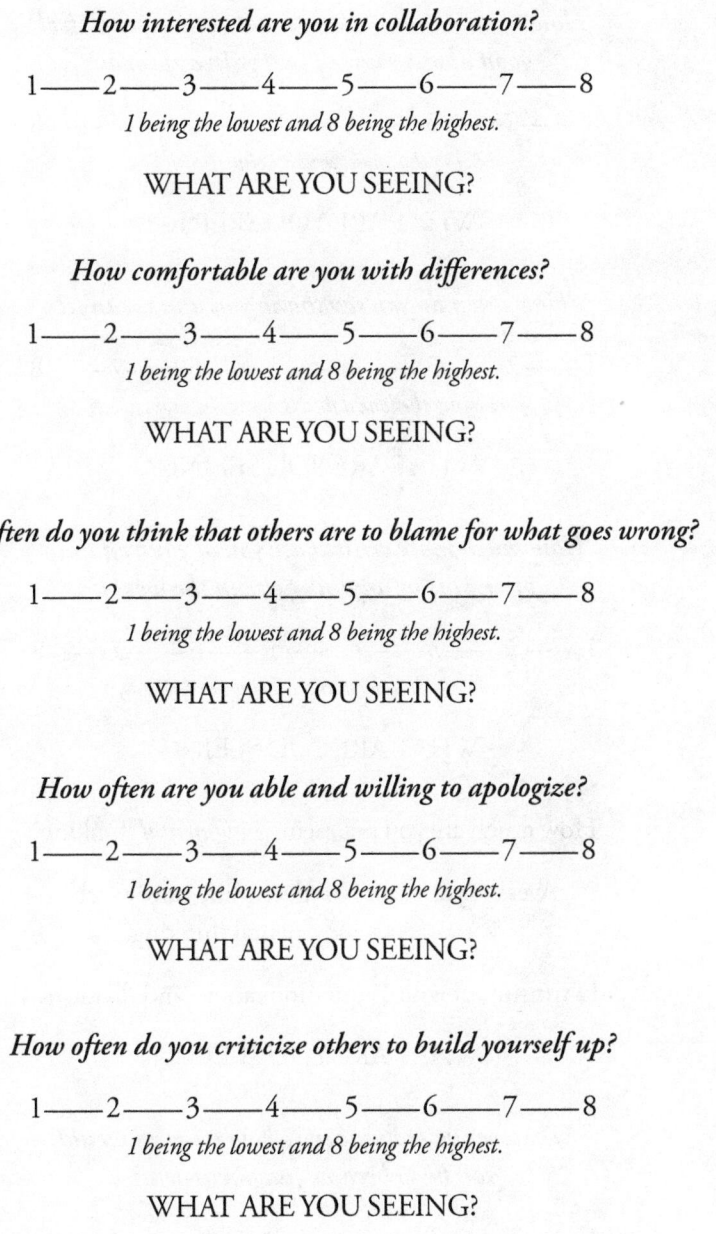

How interested are you in collaboration?

1——2——3——4——5——6——7——8
1 being the lowest and 8 being the highest.

WHAT ARE YOU SEEING?

How comfortable are you with differences?

1——2——3——4——5——6——7——8
1 being the lowest and 8 being the highest.

WHAT ARE YOU SEEING?

How often do you think that others are to blame for what goes wrong?

1——2——3——4——5——6——7——8
1 being the lowest and 8 being the highest.

WHAT ARE YOU SEEING?

How often are you able and willing to apologize?

1——2——3——4——5——6——7——8
1 being the lowest and 8 being the highest.

WHAT ARE YOU SEEING?

How often do you criticize others to build yourself up?

1——2——3——4——5——6——7——8
1 being the lowest and 8 being the highest.

WHAT ARE YOU SEEING?

*How often do you seek external validation to feel
good about yourself and gain approval?*

1——2——3——4——5——6——7——8
1 being the lowest and 8 being the highest.

WHAT ARE YOU SEEING?

How often do you say thank you and mean it?

1——2——3——4——5——6——7——8
1 being the lowest and 8 being the highest.

WHAT ARE YOU SEEING?

*How much more critical are you of yourself than
of anyone or anything else in the world?*

1——2——3——4——5——6——7——8
1 being the lowest and 8 being the highest.

WHAT ARE YOU SEEING?

How much are you practicing *judgmental* thinking?

Average your scores to determine how much
you practice judgmental thinking.

Add the sum of your 11 questions above and divide by 11.

WHAT ARE YOU SEEING?

*Whatever your number… how relieved would
you be to become judgment-free?*

1——2——3——4——5——6——7——8
1 being the lowest and 8 being the highest.

WHAT ARE YOU SEEING?

Potential-Realized Performers are judgment-free thinkers. Many maintain being judgment-free has given them the space to express Performance Energy and reach their performance potential. Judgment-free thinking liberates them from *dissonant energy,* free of reproach, denunciation, and condemnation. To them, judgment-free thinking is open-minded, fair-minded, and balanced. Judgment is a thought.

> *"When you change what you're thinkin',*
> *you will change what you're doin;..."*

Being Judgment-Free

The Potential-Realized Performers with whom I worked shifted from focusing on others to focusing on themselves. They understood that when you're judgment-free, you're able to focus inward, becoming reflective, mindful, and conscious.

What does focusing inward mean to you?

REFLECTION 97

How often are you reflective, mindful or conscious?

1——2——3——4——5——6——7——8
1 being the lowest and 8 being the highest.

WHAT ARE YOU SEEING?

When focusing on yourself and becoming introspective, there is no space for diminishing others, as confidence comes from within, and judgment—of self and others—becomes meaningless.

REFLECTION 98

How often does your confidence come from external sources?

1——2——3——4——5——6——7——8
1 being the lowest and 8 being the highest.

WHAT ARE YOU SEEING?

How often does your confidence come from within?

1——2——3——4——5——6——7——8
1 being the lowest and 8 being the highest.

WHAT ARE YOU SEEING?

When your focus is not on judging others, you no longer need to find fault or blame. Differences become stimulating, which makes room for curiosity, creativity, and collaboration. Your ways of being and behaving become determined, purposeful and intentional.

REFLECTION 99

How curious are you?

1——2——3——4——5——6——7——8
1 being the lowest and 8 being the highest.

WHAT ARE YOU SEEING?

How creative are you?

1——2——3——4——5——6——7——8
1 being the lowest and 8 being the highest.

WHAT ARE YOU SEEING?

How much is collaboration present in your life?

1——2——3——4——5——6——7——8
1 being the lowest and 8 being the highest.

WHAT ARE YOU SEEING?

Potential-Realized Performers became responsible and accountable. They said what they meant and meant what they said. They were released from thinking comparatively and competitively toward others and began to compare and compete with themselves. Soon they were able to stand on their own merits.

REFLECTION 100

What does it mean for you to be accountable and responsible?

How often do you take responsibility for your words and behaviors?

1——2——3——4——5——6——7——8
1 being the lowest and 8 being the highest.

WHAT ARE YOU SEEING?

How often do you compare and compete with others?

1——2——3——4——5——6——7——8
1 being the lowest and 8 being the highest.

WHAT ARE YOU SEEING?

Gratitude is fundamental to judgment-free thinking. Potential-Realized Performers are filled with gratitude. It is difficult to be critical, blameful, accusatory, prejudicial, or hateful when feeling grateful.

REFLECTION 101

Identify someone or something you're feeling judgmental about in a current work situation.

How much gratitude are you experiencing?

1——2——3——4——5——6——7——8
1 being the lowest and 8 being the highest.

WHAT ARE YOU SEEING?

Identify someone or something you're feeling grateful for in a current work situation.

How much judgment are you experiencing?

1——2——3——4——5——6——7——8
1 being the lowest and 8 being the highest.

WHAT ARE YOU SEEING?

Potential-Realized Performers have learned that gratitude thwarts judgment. The gratitude in judgment-free thinking brings out generosity and thoughts about collaboration, allowing everyone's performance potential to be realized. These thoughts may be the best parts of Performance Energy; you become flexible, fun, and supportive. Your blocked creativity is released. You become greater than you ever imagined.

I do believe that the essence of judgment-free thinking is described best in song when the Beatles sing, "Let it be, let it be, speaking words of wisdom, let it be."

Judgment-free thinking is all about acceptance—acceptance of others, yes, but most profoundly, acceptance of self. In my work with performers challenged by dissonant energy and unable to realize their performance potential, I have found that at the root of their judgment is self-disapproval and at worst, self-contempt and loathing. Potential- Realized Performers accept themselves and have no need to think judgmentally.

Many performers with whom I worked became aware that what they were judging in others was actually behaviors or characteristics that they themselves possessed and didn't like.

George, an actor, was highly judgmental of his director for being so bossy—the very behavior that his wife, Alice, criticized him about.

Christie, a singer, was very judgmental of a tenor with whom she was performing for occasionally burping, triggering an ugly recollection of her father who ridiculed her when she burped.

When speaking of judgment, a beautifully spiritual bassoonist reversed the Golden Rule and said, "I wouldn't want to do unto others what I wouldn't want others to do unto me."

Potential- Realized Performers are understanding and accepting— accepting differences rather than trying to change them.

To understand your judgmental-thinking style, you had the opportunity to practice 11 Judgmental -Thinking Scales. I'd now like to offer you a similar opportunity with a series of Judgment-free Thinking Scales. Increasing your awareness of your ability to be more open provides a venue for change.

REFLECTION 102

Judgment-free Thinking Scales

How often do you feel judged?

1——2——3——4——5——6——7——8
1 being the lowest and 8 being the highest.

WHAT ARE YOU SEEING?

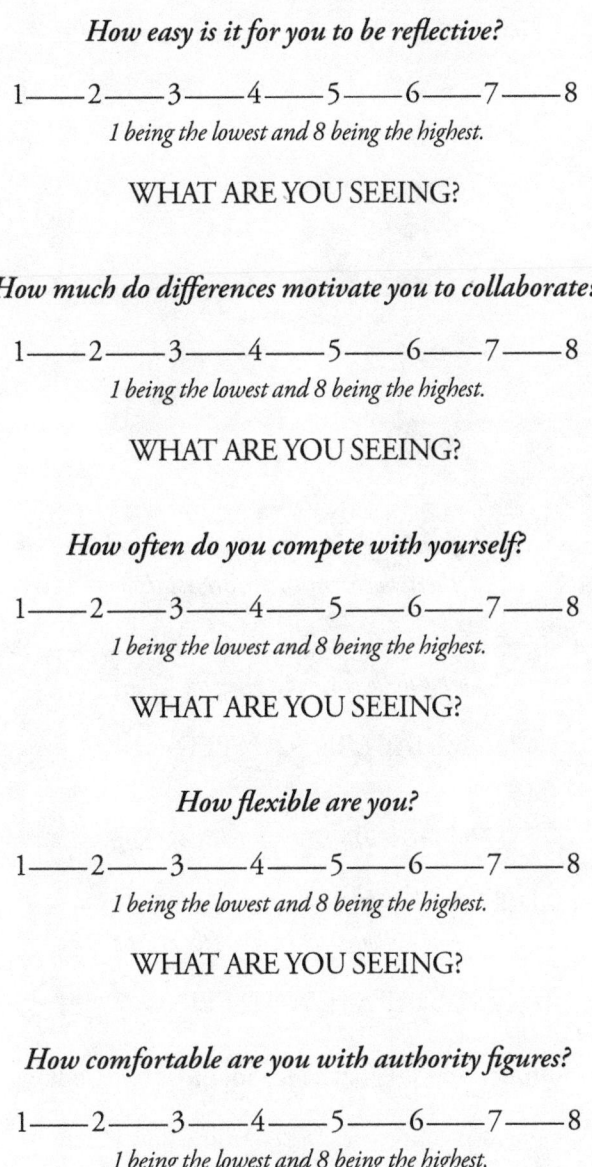

How easy is it for you to be reflective?

1——2——3——4——5——6——7——8
1 being the lowest and 8 being the highest.

WHAT ARE YOU SEEING?

How much do differences motivate you to collaborate?

1——2——3——4——5——6——7——8
1 being the lowest and 8 being the highest.

WHAT ARE YOU SEEING?

How often do you compete with yourself?

1——2——3——4——5——6——7——8
1 being the lowest and 8 being the highest.

WHAT ARE YOU SEEING?

How flexible are you?

1——2——3——4——5——6——7——8
1 being the lowest and 8 being the highest.

WHAT ARE YOU SEEING?

How comfortable are you with authority figures?

1——2——3——4——5——6——7——8
1 being the lowest and 8 being the highest.

WHAT ARE YOU SEEING?

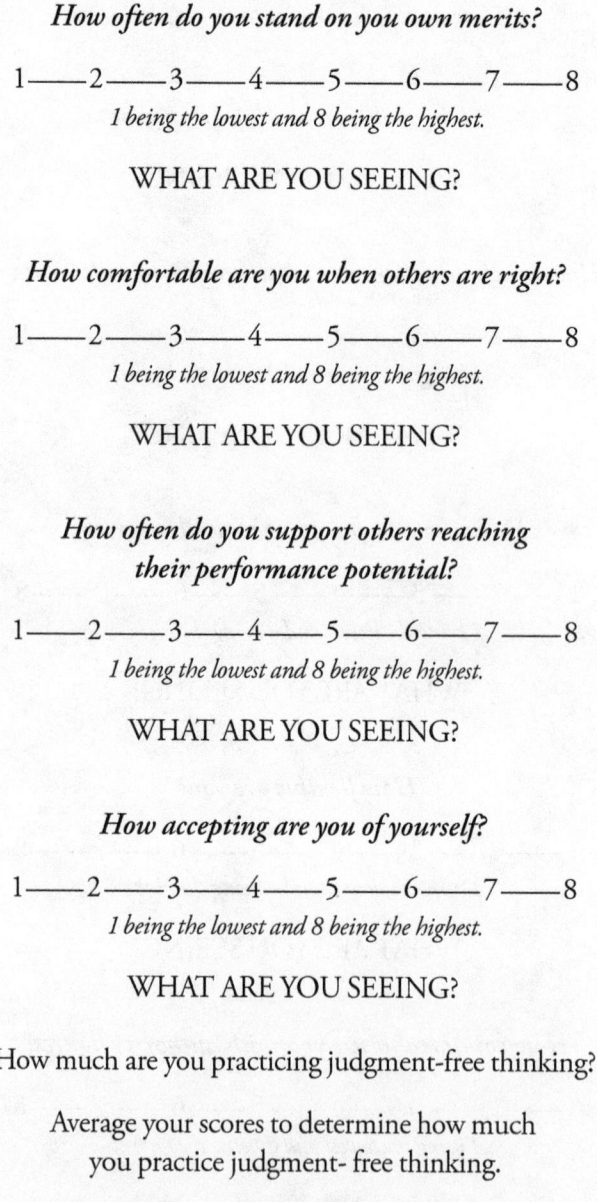

How often do you stand on you own merits?

1——2——3——4——5——6——7——8
1 being the lowest and 8 being the highest.

WHAT ARE YOU SEEING?

How comfortable are you when others are right?

1——2——3——4——5——6——7——8
1 being the lowest and 8 being the highest.

WHAT ARE YOU SEEING?

*How often do you support others reaching
their performance potential?*

1——2——3——4——5——6——7——8
1 being the lowest and 8 being the highest.

WHAT ARE YOU SEEING?

How accepting are you of yourself?

1——2——3——4——5——6——7——8
1 being the lowest and 8 being the highest.

WHAT ARE YOU SEEING?

How much are you practicing judgment-free thinking?

Average your scores to determine how much
you practice judgment- free thinking.

Add the sum of your responses to the above
10 questions and divide by 10

WHAT ARE YOU SEEING?

SANDY

Sandy had been in therapy for about four months, and, frankly, we were going in circles. At that point in my career Diva, my beautiful, ladylike, white Bichon, would often sit on my lap in my office with me. Sandy would say, "Oh, I see you have your mangy dog with you again today," or "You have that mutt with you," and occasionally he would pat her on her head.

One day, in about the seventh month of his therapy, he said, "Hey, where's that pup of yours? I miss her." I was so taken aback by his slight expression of loss that a tear trickled down my cheek. Sandy stared at me in shock, paused and said, "She's dead, isn't she?" We must've cried together for five or ten minutes. Not very professional, I know. However, that's the moment Sandy began to talk about his losses, his loneliness, and his isolation. He told me how he'd feared offending the only constant in his life, his teacher. He was afraid that if he were positive or even a bit cheerful, he would lose his teacher.

Sandy played on my office stage for the next three months and would then translate his music into words on my couch. We came to believe that the reason his sounds on his instrument were so very sweet is because he put all of his "light"—his optimism—into his trombone. He met a woman, adopted a dog, and indeed the rest of his life became sweeter as well. With judgment-free thinking, Sandy become a Potential-Realized Performer.

Depersonalized Thinking

REFLECTION 103

How often do you hear, "Don't take everything so personally!"
or "It's not personal!"?

1——2——3——4——5——6——7——8
1 being the lowest and 8 being the highest.

How often do you take it personally?

1——2——3——4——5——6——7——8
1 being the lowest and 8 being the highest.

WHAT ARE YOU SEEING?

Potential- Realized Performers think DEPERSONALIZED thoughts, code for *nothing can hurt your feelings*. They know that DEPERSONALIZED thinking frees them from taking anything personally because it's *not about them*.

Depersonalized Questions

1. In what ONE area of your work life are you taking things personally?

2. In what ONE area of your personal life are you taking things personally?

3. How would YOU show up on all the stages of your life if this were not your thinking?

"When you change what your thinkin'
you can change what you're doin"

Problem-Ridden, Pugnacious and some Promising Performers think, "*It's all about me.*" Their dissonant energy keeps them so self- absorbed that they are unable to focus on anyone other than themselves.

> **Detached Involvement** (adj.): unbiased, impersonal, emotionally removed, unemotional, separated. (n.) connection, concern, commitment, engagement, interest.

Potential-Realized Performers practice detached involvement, which sounds like an oxymoron. With detached involvement, they maintain unbiased, unemotional connection, and interest. With detached involvement, they manage and limit their subjectivity and maintain boundaries; they think with neutrality, which allows them not to take things personally.

REFLECTION 104

How new is the idea of detached involvement to you?

1——2——3——4——5——6——7——8
1 being the lowest and 8 being the highest.

WHAT ARE YOU SEEING?

Thinking with detached involvement does not mean that you do not evaluate, nor does it mean that you have to unquestioningly like something or someone. When you think with detached involvement, you can objectively listen and discuss, remaining composed and stable. You can agree to disagree. You can determine your role in a given situation and be thoughtful, realistic and wise, while maintaining your passion. Detached involvement allows you to act and perform, rationally, logically, and at the same time feel what you feel while respecting the feelings of others.

REFLECTION 105

How often do you practice detached involvement?

1——2——3——4——5——6——7——8
1 being the lowest and 8 being the highest.

WHAT ARE YOU SEEING?

Another way I refer to DEPERSONALIZED thinking is *Unbuttoning your Buttons* thinking.

Buttons are your hotspots, your Achilles heel, your triggers… the thoughts that get you all buttoned up. Potential-Realized Performers know how to unbutton their buttons.

Everyone has different buttons for different reasons.

Think about it… What do *you* take personally?

When someone interrupts you?

When you are not verbally acknowledged?

When you are not chosen?

When someone is late?

When someone whispers?

When someone gets more attention than you?

When someone doesn't do what they say they're going to do?

When your phone calls aren't returned?

REFLECTION 107

How often are your "buttons" pushed?

1——2——3——4——5——6——7——8
1 being the lowest and 8 being the highest.

WHAT ARE YOU SEEING?

When your buttons are pushed, you become completely self-centered and self-focused, taking everything that goes on—everything that is said or is happening—personally. You become mired in "all about me" thinking and behave impulsively and reactively. You create interpretations that you assign to a particular person, message or situation.

> **Interpretation** (n.): a personal way of explaining the meaning of something; thoughts to make sense of things that may or may not be related to reality. (v.) interpret—to behave or act in response to an interpretation of why something happens.

I call interpretations head stories. Head stories are inventions of the mind, a series of thoughts to make sense of things. They might or might not be related to reality. Head stories are full of dissonant energy and prevent you from reaching your performance potential. Behind every interpretation is a button.

I was in Orlando giving a Master Class for the cast of "Beauty and the Beast" where I recounted how the buttons of some of Disney's favorite villains were pushed. Both Snow White's stepmother the Queen and Gaston from "Beauty and the Beast" personalized the opinions of others, created head stories, keeping them mired in *the diva syndrome* as Pugnacious Performers.

SNOW WHITE

When the Queen looked in the mirror and heard that Snow White was the fairest of them all, she went bonkers and threw Snow White out of the castle. Imagine, if you will, that instead of taking the mirror's taste personally, she thought, *Oh, the mirror prefers Snow White's dark hair, ruby red lips and blue eyes.*

The mirror was created by a craftsperson who had the blackest hair, the palest skin, and the reddest nails in the land and the mirror was so indebted that when she looked at Snow White she remembered her creator with the most fond memories. And with that changed thought, Snow White's stepmother the Queen was able to love Snow White, her stepdaughter. And, when Snow White married, the Queen was blessed with four grandsons and one granddaughter whom she totally adored and who became her namesake and they lived happily ever after.

"When you change what you're thinkin',
you will change what you're doin;..."

BEAUTY AND THE BEAST

When Belle did not respond to Gaston's romantic advances, he threatened to kill the Beast. Imagine, had he thought, *I'm just not her type*, Gaston might have changed his behavior and gone off and fallen in love with a duchess, becoming ruler of a land where everyone paid him homage and accepted him as their leader. But choosing to take rejection personally, he ended up dead. Rather than unbuttoning his button he went down the buttonhole.

Identify two situations where your buttons have been pushed.

What head stories did you create?

TABLEAU TWENTY-TWO: GIDEON

Gideon played principal flute with his orchestra for seven years and was about to audition for a second chair in a lesser orchestra in another community because he believed that his conductor did not like him.

Why? Because she had never invited him over to her house for dinner, had never sent him a holiday card nor had she included his children at her children's birthday parties, unlike other members of the wind section.

Gideon was making an interpretation that almost cost him a position in an orchestra that he really loved. As we talked, Gideon figured out that his thinking was no more than a "head story."

How could Gideon, I mused to myself, possibly remain in the orchestra.... didn't care for him? I thought of my mantra:

> *"When you change what you're thinkin',*
> *you will change what you're doin'... "*

Head stories are often rooted in painful memories, so I asked Gideon, "When has this happened before?"

Gideon began to cry. In that moment, he realized that a button had been pushed. He asked me if I thought that his conductor was anti-Semitic.

"What do you think?" I responded.

"Well, a lot of the orchestra is Jewish, but not as ritualistic as I am. Maybe she just hates my form of Judaism. I confronted so much of this growing up."

"What's another way to think about her behavior?" I asked.

"Maybe she's being sensitive and doesn't want to offend me with a Christmas card."

Gideon looked stunned at what he had just considered. *"I've never thought about it that way."*

Three weeks later, Gideon invited his conductor out for a kosher lunch and really talked. Since then, the conductor and her family have attended Gideon's Friday night family's Shabbat dinner and Gideon's family was invited to her family's Easter egg hunt.

Gideon's head story was understandable; however, it was not only blocking his performance potential, it could have cost him his beloved job. In a recent review, I read that the flute section got a nod.

Head stories are often internalized and held inside to fester, becoming more toxic. In order to desensitize or defuse them, you want to: DE**PERSON**ALIZE, *to think differently,* **IT'S NOT ABOUT ME.**

How do you know it's a head story?

First, verbalize the head story aloud to get it out of your head.

Speak the head story to yourself and then share it with someone, preferably the person about whom you've created the head story.

Second, explore and challenge the buttons that create your head stories. Imagine… had Gideon or the Queen or Gaston realized that:

What someone does or says is about THEM…
What you do or say is about YOU…
What I do or say is about ME…
they might not have taken things personally.

Third, create an "Un-Button Your Buttons" Journal

"Un-Button Your Buttons" Journal

1. List your Buttons
2. Write your thoughts (the head story) about the people, messages or situations that pushed that Button

3. Depersonalize: Identify 5 *different* thoughts you could have to Un-button your Button.

PERSONALIZED THOUGHTS

Buttons	Head Stories	Depersonalized Thoughts
Competition		
Mirror saying Snow White is the most beautiful	I'm not the fairest in the land.	Beauty is in the eye of the beholder.
	Nobody thinks I'm beautiful anymore.	Her heart is so good, who cares.
	I'm aging.	I'm a good person.
	I'll be cut out of the will.	The relationship is more important
		Who cares what a mirror thinks.

Here's a clue about when to journal:

> Whenever your feelings are hurt, chances are a button has been pushed. Potential-Realized Performers rarely experience hurt feelings. They know that "everything is not all about me" as they're free from taking things personally.

How transformational is this repertoire
of four ways of thinking?

"When you change what you're thinkin',
you will change what you're doin'…"

I hope by now my mantra is part of your thinking repertoire, or perhaps it's even become your mantra too.

REFLECTION 107

*How much would your performance potential
be realized if your thinking was*

process-focused,

possibility-driven,

judgment-free and

depersonalized?

1——2——3——4——5——6——7——8

1 being the lowest and 8 being the highest.

WHAT ARE YOU SEEING?

FROM THE HEAD TO THE HEART – FEELINGS

It's time to give your mind a rest and let your heart do the work.

Think for a moment about an artist whom you truly love. How many of you chose this artist because he, she, or they touched your heart?

Potential-Realized Performers understand that their feelings are one of the greatest resources that enhances their Performance Energy and empowers their performance potential. Although they are aware that feelings do not define reality, as feelings are not facts, they know that feelings give that "special" quality to a performance.

Everyone goes to school to learn how to think, but how many of you go to school to learn how to *feel?*

In both my private practice and my Master Classes, I am constantly reminded of how neglected and avoided feelings are. Performers and participants often devalue and dismiss feelings. Their significance as a critical, central, crucial human and artistic resource is not understood.

REFLECTION 108

How often are you aware of your feelings?

1——2——3——4——5——6——7——8
1 being the lowest and 8 being the highest.

WHAT ARE YOU SEEING?

Many performers with whom I work had no idea what feelings really are… and furthermore, confused them with what I call feeling states as well as with thoughts.

Before understanding the vital role that feelings play in performance potential, it's important to understand feelings.

How do you define feelings?

> **Feelings:** A terrible disease that has plagued mankind since the beginning of time. Characterized by: inability to think straight, throbbing heart, acting idiotic, nausea, anxiety, and butterflies, etc. May result in: changing image/lifestyle, heartbreak, mistakes, relationships, life-altering decisions, etc.
>
> *Girl: I think I've got an awful case of feelings.*
>
> *Doctor: I'll prescribe chocolates and chick-flicks daily until your feelings are gone.*

Feelings (n.): An affect; the emotional side of someone's character; an emotional state or reaction.

I define feelings as the heart's DNA. Feelings are internal resources that give life meaning. Although feelings are experienced differently, everyone experiences the same feelings, at different times. Feelings are your heart's means of self-expression; they make you identifiable. Feelings provide color, tone, and dimension. They give everyone their personal, artistic, and vocational signature. They make everyone unique. However, feelings can be quite overwhelming.

A horn player once told me that when he begins to cry, he worries he will never stop. A pianist shared that when she's afraid, she wants to go under the covers and never come out again. A harpist explained that when she's angry, she almost wants to kill. And a dancer confided in me that when she's joyful she almost tries not to be because she knows it will end. Feelings are powerful, which makes it easy to understand why they are devalued and dismissed. Yet, everyone needs to learn how to use and manage their feelings, as feelings are such an indispensable, valuable part of us all.

I divide human feelings into four groups: mad, glad, sad and scared.

These four groups encompass a vast range of feelings and the different ways we express them. For example, when I am mad, I could also be annoyed; when I'm sad, I could say that I'm feeling depressed. I may feel happy when I'm glad and terrified when I'm scared.

Write 5 feeling words that you associate with MAD....

1.

2.

3.

4.

5.

You might have considered words like angry, irate, livid, irritated, exasperated, furious, incensed, provoked, harassed, enraged.

REFLECTION 109

How comfortable are you expressing MAD?

1——2——3——4——5——6——7——8
1 being the lowest and 8 being the highest.

WHAT ARE YOU SEEING?

What artist, when he, she, or they deliver a song, appears in a film or on TV, renders a dance or theater piece, or performs a piece of classical music or opera, elicits *anger* from you?

Write 5 feeling words that you associate with SAD…

1.

2.

3.

4.

5.

You might have considered unhappy, depressed, down, melancholy, miserable, dejected, glum, gloomy, low, despondent, morose.

REFLECTION 110

How comfortable are you expressing SAD?

1——2——3——4——5——6——7——8
1 being the lowest and 8 being the highest.

WHAT ARE YOU SEEING?

What artist, when he, she, or they deliver a song, appears in a film or on TV, renders a dance or theater piece, or performs a piece of classical music or opera, elicits *sadness* from you?

Write 5 feeling words that you associate with GLAD...

1.

2.

3.

4.

5.

You might have considered jovial, pleased, happy, joyful, gleeful, jolly, delighted, merry, content, lucky, blissful, ecstatic

---

REFLECTION 111

How comfortable are you expressing GLAD?

1——2——3——4——5——6——7——8
1 being the lowest and 8 being the highest.

WHAT ARE YOU SEEING?

What artist, when he, she, or they deliver a song, appears in a film or on TV, renders a dance or theater piece, or performs a piece of classical music or opera, elicits *happiness* from you?

Write 5 feeling words that you associate with SCARED…

1.

2.

3.

4.

5.

You might have considered frightened, terrified, fearful, afraid, petrified, worried, anxious, timid.

REFLECTION 112

How comfortable are you expressing SCARED?

1——2——3——4——5——6——7——8
1 being the lowest and 8 being the highest.

WHAT ARE YOU SEEING?

What artist, when he, she, or they deliver a song, appears in a film or on TV, renders a dance or theater piece, or performs a piece of classical music or opera, elicits *fear* from you?

REFLECTION 113

How comfortable are you expressing your feelings?

1——2——3——4——5——6——7——8
1 being the lowest and 8 being the highest.

WHAT ARE YOU SEEING?

"Feeling states" and how to distinguish them from feelings.

I created the concept of feeling states because many performers with whom I was working described themselves as emotional and yet I did not hear them talking about their *feelings*. These performers were actually internalizing their feelings and behaving in ways that were causing them to be Problem-Ridden, Pugnacious, or Promising Performers.

I was listening to the words they were using and became convinced that they thought they were expressing feelings, when they were really expressing what I began to refer to as *feeling states.*

FEELING STATES

An expression, somewhere between an experience and a feeling; often confused as an emotional presentation.

Examples of a feeling state are being relaxed, relieved, satisfied, responsible, safe, uncomfortable, exhausted, confused, distracted, alarmed, proud, disgusted, devastated, free, overwhelmed, lazy, etc.

Performers will sit on my couch and say, "*I feel so exhausted.*" And I'll ask again, *What are you feeling?* They'll repeat, "*Exhausted,*" looking at me like I need a hearing aid. Exhaustion is an experience, it is a feeling state and masks feelings.

When you become conscious of your feeling states, you can shift into feelings—you shift into mad, sad, glad, or scared and their variations.

A feeling state can encompass many disparate feelings. For example, when you say you feel responsible, you might be feeling *scared* of the responsibility, *angry* that you have to be responsible, and/or honored and therefore *happy* that you have been given the responsibility.

When you get to your feelings, the experience is different. It's visceral. Your body language changes, and you're more vulnerable and more authentic, both onstage and off.

I have found that lazy and uncomfortable are feeling states that I frequently hear in my office. As we work to "feel it through," we find that what they are feeling is anxiety. When performers uncover that they are scared, they can then choose to feel the fear and still perform the activity about which they are anxious.

Everyone speaks in feeling states. They are wonderful conveyors of information about where you are in life. *I am overwhelmed, I am proud.* It's only when you confuse them and think you are expressing actual feelings that they complicate and compromise communication.

In this way, feeling states can be very complex and may prevent you from experiencing a deeper understanding of self. Expressing feelings enables you to move closer to yourself and others. Feelings enrich emotional life, unlike feeling states which transition between experience and feelings. Working with feeling states is a dig down to the gut to get to the heart.

Both are valid, both are necessary. However, it's important to understand the difference and choose when and what you want to express. The concept is so nuanced and subtle, yet it has been very important and powerful for the artists with whom I work and is a big part of the Potential-Realized Performer's repertoire.

REFLECTION 114

*How often do you communicate in feeling states
believing that you're expressing a feeling?*

1——2——3——4——5——6——7——8
1 being the lowest and 8 being the highest.

WHAT ARE YOU SEEING?

How to differentiate thoughts from feelings.

Feelings are often confused with thoughts.

When I hear the following statements: *I feel like* or *I feel that…* I know that a *thought* is going to be expressed. *Feel like* and *feel that* are thoughts masquerading as feelings. *Feel like and feel that* are different ways of saying, *I think*. Because they have the word 'feel' in them, thoughts are often confused with feelings. Just like feeling states, *I feel like* and *I feel that* preclude performers from expressing their feelings and reaching their performance potential.

I feel like it's going to rain.

What feeling has been expressed? Mad, sad, glad or scared?
What do you feel when you think it's going to rain?
Are you mad, sad, glad or scared?
"I think it's going to rain and I'm happy about it!"

I feel that you don't like me.

What feeling has been expressed? Mad, sad, glad or scared?
What do you *feel* when you *think* that I don't like you?
Are you mad, sad, glad or scared?
"I think that you don't like me, and it frightens me."

A performer with whom I worked told me that when he confused his thoughts with feelings he was really intellectualizing his feelings.

When you think you are expressing your feelings, when you think you are being emotional but you're not, you deprive yourself of a vital human resource. You're not truly in touch with your inner self.

When thoughts are accepted as feelings, you remain in your head and disconnected from your heart. As a performer, this can have dire consequences as you are not emotionally involved with your script, the flavors of your music, the intimacy of your cast, your work environment, family or friends, regardless of the tasks at hand. Only your mind is working, and you're unable to open your heart and express your sensibilities, sensitivities and vulnerabilities.

REFLECTION 115

*How often do you say 'I feel like' or 'I feel that'
believing that you're expressing a feeling?*

1——2——3——4——5——6——7——8
1 being the lowest and 8 being the highest.

WHAT ARE YOU SEEING?

Feelings and Accomplishment

Everyone needs to be acknowledged, it's a human need and want. I learned from the Potential-Realized Performers with whom I work that there's a special feeling attached to every performance accomplishment.

When you understand feelings and feeling states, and are able to differentiate between feelings and thoughts, you are eager and able to identify a special feeling that you associate with your performance achievements.

As you hold Hamlet's mirror you will learn that this feeling is different for everyone. It plays a major role in Performance Energy and reaching your performance potential. Identifying this special feeling is a wonderful gift to yourself.

How do you identify that special feeling?

_____

PERFORMANCE GOALS!

Action goals—specific, tangible, external goals—achieved
and accomplished onstage, in the pit, in audition, rehearsal,
lessons, in any areas that pertain to the performing arts.

_____

Number 1: Write a performance goal that you can identify at this very moment.

Begin your performance goal with *I WILL* to demonstrate intention, aim and purpose.

For example:

I WILL wake up at 6 am and work out to lose seven pounds.

I WILL stop complaining and practice at least one hour a day for the next four weeks.

I WILL stop wasting time on social media and focus on my work.

I WILL be more prepared each day.

I WILL warm up for 30 minutes before each rehearsal and performance.

I WILL create three back-stories for my character and come onstage with a different one for each night.

I WILL go out with my colleagues once a week to move out of my shy comfort zone.

I WILL clean myself up to look more presentable to get hired.

I WILL practice my Notable Reflections daily.

I WILL, as a Broadway performer reminded me, do as Peter Pan directed, and think three lovely thoughts every day.

I Will....

Number 2: Write ONE feeling that you WILL have when you accomplish your performance goal.

When I accomplish this performance goal, *I WILL feel...*

Look at your performance goal to make certain it's what you really want.

Surprise! Your response to number 2, your feeling, is your true performance goal, *what you really want*. And, once identified, Potential-Realized Performers understood that this special feeling can be with you, and you can draw on it, whenever and wherever you are.

Whatever you wrote for number 1—your performance goal—is your approach, your external strategy, your plan, your action… the way to get to your special feeling.

That special feeling, your heart's desire, whatever you identified, be it joy, excitement, calm, awe, relief, happiness…whatever you associated and connected with your performance achievement, enables you to tune into and turn on your Performance Energy and realize your performance potential.

Ironically, it is not the success of the performance that creates Performance Energy, it is your special *feeling* about achieving that goal.

TABLEAU TWENTY-THREE: FRANCIS

Francis was convinced that he would never gain the weight that he needed to play Nathan in "Guys and Dolls." So, we set upon a goal of eating 4,000 calories a day for two months, and identifying the special feeling associated with accomplishing this performance goal. Francis had a history of not completing what he started. Yet, he had wanted to do Nathan since he was a little boy because his father had performed the role before him. It actually took him three months to gain thirty-seven lbs. and reach his goal.

Francis first identified shock, which was a feeling-state. In our work he gained an awareness that his shock was connected to his special feeling, ecstasy. Francis amazed himself. He had turned his life around. He told me his wife, who didn't much care for the extra weight, said that he even followed through on carrying out the trash. As he started to trust himself to believe that he could follow through on things, his confidence rose. When he decided to do something new he believed that he would accomplish it. Others also began to trust him.

When "Guys and Dolls" closed, to make his wife happy, Francis went on a diet. Remembering how ecstatic he'd felt when accomplishing his last performance goal, Francis lost the weight. He carried his ecstasy with him throughout his life, and, three years later, he was ecstatic over the birth of his twins.

In the moment, *now*, you can experience Performance Energy.

You can use your special feeling to bring your performance potential to life at any time. Write your responses to the following questions:

1. My special feeling is:

2. What did you achieve *today* that can cause you to experience your special feeling?

3. What can you think about yourself right now for you to awaken your special feeling?

4. What opportunity do you need to create for yourself to enjoy your special feeling?

5. What choice do you need to make to sustain your special feeling?

When Potential-Realized Performers do the heart's work, and create a performance goal *I WILL...* to embrace their special feeling, they set themselves up to experience Performance Energy and fulfill the possibility within them each and every day.

PERFORMANCE CHARACTERISTICS

Potential-Realized Performers possess and demonstrate eight performance characteristics that I refer to as an Octave of Hi Cs. I observed the following Hi Cs resounding in performers who were consistently reaching their performance potential: Consciousness, Civility, Commitment, Confidence, Curiosity, Creativity, Calm, and Connection.

The more integrated and organic each Hi C is, the more Performance Energy is available, and the more immune you are to *the diva syndrome,* and being stuck.

The beauty is that everyone can learn this octave, and when tuning into it, anything can be accomplished.

Each of the eight performance characteristics has its own set of overtones.

> **Overtone** (n.): a musical tone that is a part of the harmonic series above a fundamental note and may be heard with it. A secondary effect, quality, or meaning.

For many years, I have been identifying overtones that are connected to each of the eight performance characteristics and have attempted to make each overtone as relevant as possible.

CONSCIOUSNESS
Overtones: awareness, mindfulness, responsiveness, openness, focus, attentiveness, alertness, meaning, clarity.

CIVILITY
Overtones: responsibility, accountability, courtesy, respect, graciousness, dignity, honor, poise, manners.

COMMITMENT
Overtones: engagement, vulnerability, dedication, passion, purpose, generosity, loyalty, trustworthiness, enthusiasm.

CONFIDENCE
Overtones: self-esteem, authenticity, gracefulness, freedom from judgment, resilience, basic trust, empowerment.

CURIOSITY

Overtones: exploration, understanding, discovery, freedom, communication, possibility, opportunity.

CREATIVITY

Overtones: expressivity, intuition, inspiration, resilience, virtuosity, genius, reinvention, innovation, vision, humor.

CALM

Overtones: inner-peace, empathy, satisfaction, pleasure, joy, gratitude, bliss.

CONNECTION

Overtones: synergy, collaboration, charisma, oneness, interdependence, relatedness, compatibility, fun.

You, of course, may associate a completely different and equally valid overtone with the same Hi C. Feel free to do this at will and whim or to interchange overtones from one Hi C to another.

*How do you increase your experience and expression
of each performance characteristic?*

I've created an instrument to help you measure how much you are experiencing and expressing each performance characteristic. The instrument is called *The Performance Potential Hi C Wheel.* And although the work of the wheel may be challenging, working the Wheel can be fun.

The Wheel is designed to create nine Performance Potential profiles and is worked in two stages. The first stage involves creating one Performance Potential profile for each of the Hi C's.

Each spoke on the Wheel represents one of the Hi C's. When scaled, each of the Hi C's reflects your Performance Potential in that area.

WORKING THE WHEEL

Instructions – Stage 1

On a scale of 1—10 for each of the Hi Cs:

Circle the number that best represents how much you value each Hi C at this moment.

1 = not at all   10 = totally

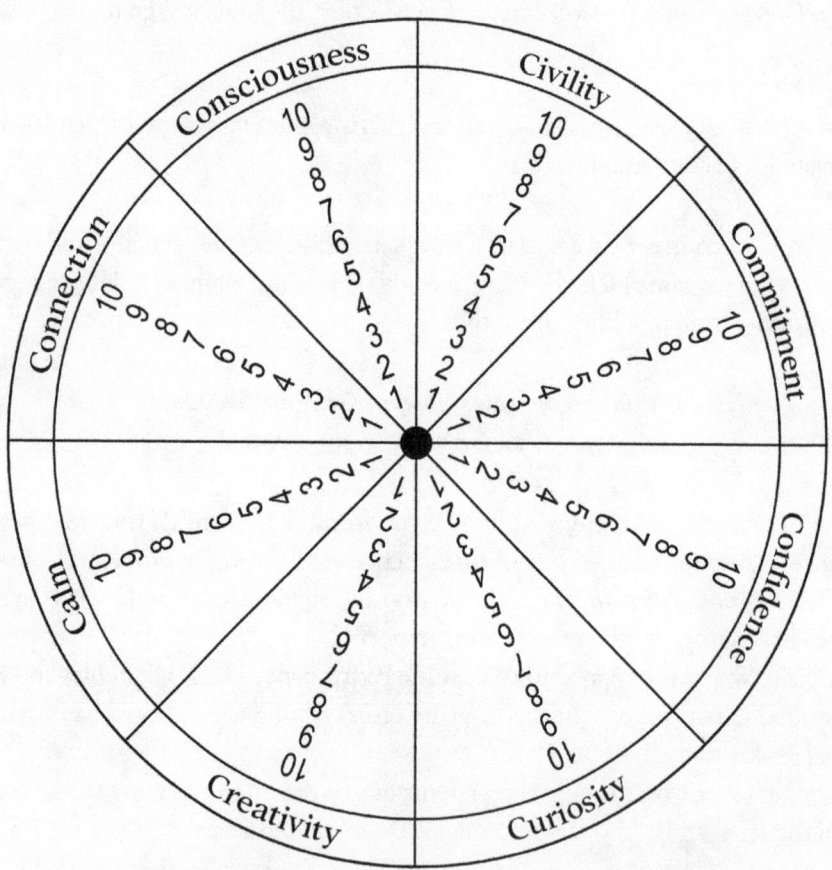

The meaning of each of the eight performance characteristics will be very personal to you and hold its own definition. For example, one definition of confidence is: *self-assurance arising from one's appreciation of one's own abilities or qualities*. However, your definition of confidence may include your own reflections, memories or experiences. This is true for all the other performance characteristics as well. Each meaning is unique unto you.

Let's have some fun and work your first Wheel. You might want to make a separate copy of the Wheel before you begin.

Stage 1:

CONSCIOUSNESS

Overtones: awareness, mindfulness, responsiveness, openness, focus, attentiveness, alertness, meaning, clarity

Circle the number on your Wheel that best represents how much you value Consciousness at this moment.

> What would be different if that number was one or two numbers higher (or lower)?

> What do you want to do to make that happen?

CIVILITY

Overtones: responsibility, accountability, courtesy, respect, graciousness, dignity, honor, poise, manners

Circle the number on your Wheel that best represents how much you value Civility at this moment.

> What would be different if that number was one or two numbers higher (or lower)?

> What do you want to do to make that happen?

COMMITMENT

Overtones: engagement, vulnerabity, dedication, passion, purpose, generosity, loyalty, trustworthiness, enthusiasm

Circle the number on your Wheel that best represents how much you value Commitment at this moment.

> What would be different if that number was one or two numbers higher (or lower)?

> What do you want to do to make that happen?

CONFIDENCE

Overtones: self-esteem, authenticity, gracefulness, freedom from judgment, resilience, basic trust, empowerment.

Circle the number on your Wheel that best represents how much you value Confidence at this moment.

> What would be different if that number was one or two numbers higher (or lower)?

> What do you want to do to make that happen?

CURIOSITY

Overtones: exploration, understanding, discovery, freedom, communication, possibility, opportunity

Circle the number on your Wheel that best represents how much you value Curiosity at this moment.

What would be different if that number was one or two numbers higher (or lower)?

What do you want to do to make that happen?

CREATIVITY

Overtones: expressivity, intuition, inspiration, resilience, virtuosity, genius, reinvention, innovation, vision, humor

Circle the number on your Wheel that best represents how much you value Creativity at this moment.

What would be different if that number was one or two numbers higher (or lower)?

What do you want to do to make that happen?

CALM

Overtones: inner-peace, empathy, satisfaction, pleasure, joy, gratitude, bliss

Circle the number on your Wheel that best represents how much you value Calm at this moment.

What would be different if that number was one or two numbers higher (or lower)?

What do you want to do to make that happen?

Connection

Overtones: synergy, collaboration, charisma, oneness, interdependence, relatedness, compatibility, fun

Circle the number on your Wheel that best represents how much you value Connection at this moment.

> What would be different if that number was one or two numbers higher (or lower)?

> What do you want to do to make that happen?

You have now created eight Performance Potential profiles.

Instructions – Stage 2

Draw a line that connects one circled Performance Potential number to another circled Performance Potential number so that they are all connected to create your ninth profile, a visualization of how much overall Performance Potential you are experiencing and expressing.

Performance Characteristic Questions

1. What is meaningful to you about your overall Performance Potential profile?

2. What surprised you the most?

3. Which individual profile is the most meaningful?

4. What causes it to be meaningful?

5. What have you achieved today that raised or lowered a performance characteristic?

6. How might you want to use the Wheel in the future?

 – "Work" the Wheel: daily, weekly, monthly, etc.?

 – Focus on a specific Hi C?

 – Focus on aligning your Hi C balance?

REFLECTION 116

How much fun did you have Working the Wheel?

1——2——3——4——5——6——7——8
1 being the lowest and 8 being the highest.

WHAT ARE YOU SEEING?

One of the highlights of Working the Wheel is that, at a glance, you will see both at a Hi C and overall Performance Potential level where you are in alignment and/or choose where you want to be.

DIVINE DIVA BEHAVIORS

Potential-Realized Performers express what I call Divine Diva behaviors.

DIVINE DIVA BEHAVIOR

An action, performance, comportment or demeanor that restores the diva to her historical divine status and her grace-filled standing.

As you hold Hamlet's mirror, how do you see these behaviors reflected in yourself?

1. Potential-Realized Performers choose.

Potential-Realized Performers practice their power of conscious choice. They are acutely aware and have an elevated state of consciousness. And, where being *aware* shows up powerfully is in the area of *choice*.

> **Choice** (n.): a range of possibilities from which one or more may be selected; the *power* to *empower* your performance potential, personally and professionally.

REFLECTION 117

How aware are you that choice is a significant way to empower your performance potential?

1——2——3——4——5——6——7——8
1 being the lowest and 8 being the highest.

WHAT ARE YOU SEEING?

Potential-Realized Performers are aware that there are always **five** choices to any personal or professional activity, relationship or situation. Their awareness and their willingness to practice choice is what makes choice a Divine Diva behavior.

Power of Conscious Choice

1. Consciously choose to remain at the mercy of any personal or professional situation:

> *I am unwilling to change.*
>
> *I choose to remain a victim.*
>
> *I choose to stay stuck.*

REFLECTION 118

How often do you choose Choice #1?

1——2——3——4——5——6——7——8
1 being the lowest and 8 being the highest.

WHAT ARE YOU SEEING?

Although it may not seem to move you forward, this is empowering because unwillingness to change is a conscious choice.

2. Consciously choose to change your perspective of a personal or professional situation:

> *I will think differently about it.*
>
> *I will have a more positive and optimistic attitude.*
>
> *I will see the possibilities and opportunities.*
>
> *I will decrease my dissonant energy.*
>
> *I will reframe the situation and make lemonade out of lemons.*

REFLECTION 119

How often do you choose Choice #2?

1——2——3——4——5——6——7——8

1 being the lowest and 8 being the highest.

WHAT ARE YOU SEEING?

---

3. Consciously choose to change yourself:

I will become the change I want to see in my world.

I will show up differently in my work.

I will become aligned with who I am, what I do and how I do it.

I will gain understanding of what's stopping me.

I will practice harmonic energy.

REFLECTION 120

How often do you choose Choice #3?

1——2——3——4——5——6——7——8

1 being the lowest and 8 being the highest.

WHAT ARE YOU SEEING?

---

4. Consciously choose to accept the personal or professional situation:

I will not take things personally.

I will be judgment-free.

I will experience forgiveness and gratitude.

I will increase my harmonic energy.

REFLECTION 121

How often do you choose Choice #4?

1——2——3——4——5——6——7——8
1 being the lowest and 8 being the highest.

WHAT ARE YOU SEEING?

---

5. Consciously choose to leave the personal or professional situation:

I will let go.

I will set healthy boundaries.

I will invest in self-care.

I will understand that every leaving is a new beginning.

I will increase my harmonic energy.

REFLECTION 122

How often do you choose Choice #5?

1——2——3——4——5——6——7——8
1 being the lowest and 8 being the highest.

WHAT ARE YOU SEEING?

Everyone can consciously choose how to experience each moment of life. This is what makes choice a Divine Diva behavior.

Power of Conscious Choice

Fill out the columns below to practice your power of conscious choice.
Describe a personal or professional situation that was challenging for you.

Consciously choose your personal or professional situation	Which of the 5 *Choices* do you choose?	What will be different if you make this choice?	What has to happen to put that choice into action?
My director yelled at me	#4	I will respect myself	I need to change what I'm thinking

REFLECTION 123

How big a role does conscious choice play in your personal life?

1——2——3——4——5——6——7——8

1 being the lowest and 8 being the highest.

WHAT ARE YOU SEEING?

How big a role does conscious choice play in your work?

1——2——3——4——5——6——7——8
1 being the lowest and 8 being the highest.

WHAT ARE YOU SEEING?

2. Potential-Realized Performers are afraid, yet they show up anyway.

Potential-Realized Performers are *courageous* because they constantly step out of their terrified comfort zone. They demonstrate extreme flexibility and curiosity and will risk anything. Potential-Realized Performers are often petrified, scared to death, and yet they are fearless. They are fearless not because they are not frightened, they are fearless because they are frightened and perform anyway. This is what makes being afraid and taking action anyway a Divine Diva behavior.

TABLEAU TWENTY-FOUR: JUSTINE

"'Don't be so dramatic.' I heard this all my life growing up. All I was doing was expressing my feelings."

Justine came into therapy to learn how to be emotional as her feelings were held so tightly within… fearing her parent's scorn, judgment, and retaliation.

Justine was raised in an upper middle-class Episcopalian home. She discovered dance when she was four. "Dancing suited my family's ethic where children were to be seen and not heard, and the expression of feelings was almost sinful."

"Dance became my release and haven. Yet, emoting, even in motion, has always been risky for me."

Much to her parent's dismay, Justine showed great promise in her younger years as a dancer and progressed rapidly as a classical ballerina. Her parents supported her "dance habit" as a way to prevent emotional displays at home. They threatened to withdraw financial and any other support of her dance if she were too expressive, both onstage and off.

Therefore, in her teenage years, Justine switched to modern dance because she thought it was less emotionally expressive than classical ballet. Justine was terrified of any demonstrative display. And yes, as talented as she was, this fear followed her into her chosen profession.

Justine came into therapy when she was nineteen years old; we worked together for six years. Of course, Justine expected me to be critical of any emotional display as she had transferred her parents' judgment of her onto the whole world, including me. She would think that I was angry or judgmental if ever she showed any emotion or feeling in my office.

This changed when I developed laryngitis in the second year of our work and Justine imagined that I was critically ill. My laryngitis provided Justine the excuse to show her feelings; and expose them she did. My verbal silence—just like in dance—seemed to open her up, and she revealed all the feelings that were locked inside. It was as if somehow my inability to verbalize and find fault with her, which she had feared, allowed her to be emotional, to step outside her comfort zone and become fearless. Justine expressed, in addition to anger and sadness, much joy and a great sense of humor. We laughed as one day she marched into my office with her own box of Kleenex. She had shed so many tears.

She is now recognized and rewarded in major dance circles for her expressive style and is about to be married to someone she trusts enough to risk crying in front of when she reads her beloved poetry books.

REFLECTION 124

How fearless are you?

1——2——3——4——5——6——7——8
1 being the lowest and 8 being the highest.

WHAT ARE YOU SEEING?

How comfortable are you taking risks?

1——2——3——4——5——6——7——8
1 being the lowest and 8 being the highest.

WHAT ARE YOU SEEING?

3. Potential-Realized Performers intuit.

Potential-Realized Performers are intuitive; they manifest an inner wisdom, a unique kind of knowing. Knowing, *when you have no way of knowing what you know and how you know it!*

REFLECTION 125

How often do you meet someone who seems to immediately know and understand you?

1——2——3——4——5——6——7——8
1 being the lowest and 8 being the highest.

WHAT ARE YOU SEEING?

This is what causes intuiting to be a Divine Diva behavior.

Everyone with a profound sense of basic trust in themselves has intuition. Your intuition allows you to achieve synthesis and connection with everyone and everything. Potential-Realized Performers have told me that:

"I'm connected with myself"

"... with my art... with my work"

"... with my audiences"

"... with my senses"

"I'm in union with one and all"

Potential-Realized Performers have a charismatic, contagious connection with everyone as they are in a state of *WEness*. Their Performance Energy is like a magnet. They feel a sense of belonging and a sense of sameness with all. As actors, singers and dancers they can walk in their character's shoes and inhabit who they are, and as musicians they are able to merge with a piece of music.

Potential-Realized Performers have learned that 'WE' are all the same... all connected. Imagine what it's like to experience such relatedness, such kinship, such oneness.

REFLECTION 126

How intuitive are you?

1——2——3——4——5——6——7——8
1 being the lowest and 8 being the highest.

WHAT ARE YOU SEEING?

---

4. Potential-Realized Performers share who they are.

They want to be known. They give of themselves emotionally, intellectually, physically and creatively. Potential-Realized Performers want to spread the greatness they have within. Their Performance Energy elevates their graciousness and generosity. It's important to them to be open and vulnerable.

Potential-Realized Performers love to share their differences, eccentricities, outrageousness, and especially their 'craziness.' They love to laugh at themselves and have others laugh with them.

This Divine Diva behavior includes sharing their non-conformist and unconventional selves, which isn't always accepted or popular. However, a very outspoken actor told me that being vulnerable is "worth it. If you can't stand the heat get out of the kitchen." A musician said, "If they don't like me or my standing up to the union, too bad. I'm not a pretzel." And a comedian who could not get hired because of his controversial political opinions announced as he left the stage that he wants his tombstone to read, "I did it my way." A harpist told me that her values inform her about her choices and the people with whom she associates. A lyricist said that his values are his "moral compass, purpose and direction in life."

The passion and commitment motivating this Divine Diva behavior cannot be overestimated. Their values define them. They have the confidence and the strength to live their values every day. Everyone who recognizes this Divine Diva behavior in themselves needs to, wants to, and shares themselves on all the stages of their lives.

It's important to them to express themselves — to be open, authentic, accessible, undefended and vulnerable. Being known, warts and all, is the way that they want to be and behave. Sharing, through self-expression, is central in their lives.

REFLECTION 127

How much do you let yourself be known?

1——2——3——4——5——6——7——8
1 being the lowest and 8 being the highest.

How central is self-expression in your life?

1——2——3——4——5——6——7——8
1 being the lowest and 8 being the highest.

WHAT ARE YOU SEEING?

TABLEAU TWENTY-FIVE: HAL

Hal was the second performer I saw in my New York office. He was in a big show on Broadway and had read an article about me in the *New York Post* regarding stage fright. Hal did not have stage fright; he had life fright. This was the mid-1980s, and he had found two lesions, one on his stomach and one on his left leg. He was twenty-seven years old. I had heard the word AIDS just eight months before.

In my work, I had just begun developing the concept of Performance Potential, and as I look back, there has been no one who taught me more about this idea than Hal.

Hal's partner had died the year before and had helped us both understand, more than either of us ever wanted to, about how gay men die from this horrible disease. How to live with dying or how to live with knowing how you're going to die, was challenging.

My impulse was to not charge Hal my fee, but I decided that would be demeaning; we continued our once a week sessions. How was Hal going to reach his potential as he was dying? And for that matter, how was I, as his psychotherapist, going to reach mine?

We decided that the questions are still the same. Who am I? What are my values? What do I want? Am I living my values? This is how our work proceeded. Hal needed to leave his show because his stamina was not what the show demanded; but he did not stop performing. No indeed.

One of his life's dreams was to choreograph a show of his own and share the story of his life. For that he found the energy. His friends got together to be cast in his production and contributed money to rent a studio for two performances here in the city.

Here, the universe seemed to be smiling. Hal had rehearsed a number of duets with a friend of his on my office stage, sharing the love he had for his deceased partner. His dance was one of the most vulnerable pieces of choreography I had ever witnessed. It was all that I could do to not share my tears. Unfortunately, Hal was too weak to perform when his production went up. Hal was a member of the audience and witnessed his work. I attended the second of the two performances.

Hal died the next day, surrounded by his mother and his friends. At Hal's memorial service, they played the video of his dance. I cried my heart out.

5. Potential-Realized Performers maintain their own energy.

REFLECTION 128

How often do you enter a room feeling blue when suddenly your spirits are lifted by happy, excited people?

1——2——3——4——5——6——7——8
1 being the lowest and 8 being the highest.

WHAT ARE YOU SEEING?

How often are you in a great mood and meet a friend who is upset and depressed and suddenly you are feeling lousy?

1——2——3——4——5——6——7——8
1 being the lowest and 8 being the highest.

WHAT ARE YOU SEEING?

If you learned that you can be changed by others' emotions, you can be entrained.

Entrainment (n.): the inability to support your own energy, dissonant or harmonic; lacking your own sense of agency.

Entrain (v.) energy adapts to like energy. To abdicate your conscious choice as to what energy you want to experience and express.

When your energy is changed by an
outside force, you are entrained.

I was unaware of this wonderful word entrainment until about seven years ago when it literally changed my life.

Potential-Realized Performers are entrainment-free. Regardless of what kind of energy is around them, the energy they show up with, in whatever setting, remains stable and is not shaken. This is what causes being entrainment-free to be Divine—maintaining your own energy.

REFLECTION 129

How much do you allow yourself to be entrained?

1——2——3——4——5——6——7——8
1 being the lowest and 8 being the highest.

How much are you entrainment-free?

1——2——3——4——5——6——7——8
1 being the lowest and 8 being the highest.

WHAT ARE YOU SEEING?

---

6. Potential-Realized Performers exercise self-care.

Potential-Realized Performers know that you can't exercise power of conscious choice, be afraid yet show up anyway, share, intuit, or maintain your own energy, until you love yourself. And how do you know you love yourself? You practice self-care.

What does self-care mean to you?

List 5 ways you care for yourself.

1.

2.

3.

4.

5.

List 5 ways you want to care for yourself

1.

2.

3.

4.

5.

Exercising self-care means filling yourself with what you need and want. It means being self-filled which can often feel selfish. However, because you are able to give to yourself, you are able to give of yourself.

REFLECTION 130

How often does self-care feel selfish?

1——2——3——4——5——6——7——8
1 being the lowest and 8 being the highest.

WHAT ARE YOU SEEING?

Self-care means having strong boundaries. Potential-Realized Performers are protective of their needs and wants. They know when to say no. They know when to let go.

REFLECTION 131

How comfortable are you saying NO?

1——2——3——4——5——6——7——8
1 being the lowest and 8 being the highest.

WHAT ARE YOU SEEING?

TABLEAU TWENTY-SIX: DAVID

At seventy-one, David chose to leave a profession he dearly loved. He knew it was time to go. He came into therapy because he needed a little help in that direction. David was a jazz pianist and as he said, "Everybody knows jazz musicians can go on forever, but I want to leave while I'm still on top."

David had studied classical piano since he was seven years old and had turned to jazz in his mid-twenties. He had been divorced twice: "Not my choosing…I've never walked away from anything in my life."

Actually, jazz *was* his life. At his age, David was still performing, still recording, still on the road. "I've decided to take care of myself, not wait until they don't want me anymore, walk away and trust that the gods are smiling on me."

Ironically, letting go of the piano took place at my piano on my office stage. He played and played and played as he said goodbye to his musical career. I said very little and mostly listened. He played for about six months, when indeed the gods did smile on him, blessing David with twin grandchildren in Pensacola, Florida. He moved into his daughter's home there to care for not only himself, but also his baby granddaughters. David felt divinely cared for.

REFLECTION 132

How much do you engage in self-care?

1——2——3——4——5——6——7——8

1 being the lowest and 8 being the highest.

WHAT ARE YOU SEEING?

7. Potential-Realized Performers listen.

How often do you meet someone who really gets you?

It's easy to say, "*I hear you I hear you I heard you.*" However, with hearing, you are often in your own head thinking of what you want to say, what you want to do, what advice you want to offer, how you want to fix, how you want to contest and argue. With hearing, *it's all about me.*

REFLECTION 133

How often are you just hearing?

1——2——3——4——5——6——7——8

1 being the lowest and 8 being the highest.

WHAT ARE YOU SEEING?

REFLECTION 134

*How often do you interrupt when others are
speaking and make their story about you?*

1——2——3——4——5——6——7——8
1 being the lowest and 8 being the highest.

WHAT ARE YOU SEEING?

With listening, it's about the other. Listening is empathic. The ability to listen is a rare talent. Listening is the suspension of your personal agenda, feelings, thoughts, impulses and wants, and placing yourself in another person's reality. Listening is active. With listening, you wait for cues about where the other person wants to go in the conversation, what the other person needs to discuss, when the other person wants to be silent, if and what the other person might need from you.

REFLECTION 135

How well do you listen?

1——2——3——4——5——6——7——8
1 being the lowest and 8 being the highest.

WHAT ARE YOU SEEING?

Potential- Realized Performers practice active listening by thinking about others and focusing on what they're saying and thinking. Potential-Realized Performers are all about empathy.

8. Potential-Realized Performers learn and change.

For a Potential-Realized Performer, there is nothing more exciting than learning. Anything and everything that they can take in, they do. They find the unknown and uncertainty both interesting and intriguing—opportunities to gain knowledge. If they didn't find delight and even thrill in learning, they wouldn't be able to do what they do. I refer to everyone who manifests this Divine Diva behavior a learning sponge.

Think about it, isn't life but an opportunity to learn?

I find that Potential-Realized Performers are so comfortable with learning because they long to be stimulated, challenged, and enlightened. It's not that they are necessarily scholarly or even intellectually inclined, but I believe that it is their love of learning that causes them to embrace change. At the core of the Potential-Realized Performer's affinity for learning is a love of change. Why? Learning changes you.

REFLECTION 136

How much do you love learning?

1——2——3——4——5——6——7——8
1 being the lowest and 8 being the highest.

WHAT ARE YOU SEEING?

Potential-Realized Performers welcome change: change onstage, change in rhythms, change in dance partners, change in audience responses. Change keeps performance potential alive and dynamic.

REFLECTION 137

Performance Potential Scale

Throughout *Hamlet's Mirror*, you have been practicing the
Divine Diva behavior of learning in 136 Reflections.
How much did you learn?

1——2——3——4——5——6——7——8
1 being the lowest and 8 being the highest.

WHAT ARE YOU SEEING?

How much did you change?

1——2——3——4——5——6——7——8
1 being the lowest and 8 being the highest.

WHAT ARE YOU SEEING?

REFLECTION FINALE

Before I introduced you to the Performer Personality Profiles, I invited
you to contemplate their names and to reflect which of the four you
sensed reflected you best. After holding Hamlet's mirror, and having
deeply contemplated each profile, which one best reflects you now?

Problem-Ridden Performer
Pugnacious Performer
Promising Performer
Potential-Realized Performer

WHAT ARE YOU SEEING?

I have the rare opportunity to witness many Potential-Realized Performers with whom I work. I watch them on TV, film, and on all forms of social media. In person, I see them perform at the Met, in many NYC dance venues, on Broadway and off-Broadway stages, at Carnegie and Geffen Halls, as well as in a myriad of other performing spaces around the city. I even watch them gracefully accept acknowledgment on award shows. And it brings me such joy to see their transformations as they represent their culture, their mission, their art form, their colleagues, their families and most of all… themselves, expressing all the learning from Hamlet's artists who hold the mirror up to life.

EPILOGUE

This brings me back to the Young Woman.

TABLEAU TWENTY-SEVEN:
THE YOUNG WOMAN, TAKE THREE

Forty-eight years after the mortifying incident at The Neighborhood Playhouse with Sir John Gielgud, the Young Woman saw Sir John again in England. She was seated at a very small bar with her husband, Howard Kanefield, in a hotel called The Royal Crescent in Bath. At that time, Sir John was with Richard Thomas, as they were shooting a film together.

The Young Woman experienced a harrowing flashback. She was once again in New York in her teens, so tongue-tied that her silenced voice temporarily re-emerged. However, she called upon all that she had seen in the performers with whom she worked, maintained her harmonic energy, remained in the moment, and fearlessly used her voice to thank the great actor/director.

The Young Woman looked Sir John in the eye, held her glass of sparkling champagne high, and toasted him. She felt truly divine.

ACKNOWLEDGEMENTS:

Hamlet's Mirror is a work of love that has taken over thirty years to complete… and without the enthusiasm and wisdom of family, friends and colleagues could not have been accomplished.

There are Cindy and Jen, coaching colleagues who also became friends, whose early input provided much guidance.

There are my dear friends Annie, April, Audrey, Carol, Dan, Ellen, Julie, Laurie, Martha and Renée who were always there with a new perspective.

And of course, my wonderful Disney, Juilliard School and Lotos Club families who have been an unwavering support throughout these years.

My children and grandchildren - in particular, Jimmy, Lois, Susan, and Derek– have been my rocks.

Hamlet's Mirror is a work of collaboration, love and laughter and absolutely could not have been written without my colleague, friend, and family member by osmosis, Dianne Conjeaud.

It is impossible to acknowledge everyone who has inspired me over these three decades. In addition to the performing artists with whom I've worked, there are those who have made tremendous contributions to *Hamlet's Mirror* and those who have made small but not less meaningful ones. You know who you are. I thank you profoundly from the bottom of my heart.

CPSIA information can be obtained
at www.ICGtesting.com
Printed in the USA
JSHW052327240722
28386JS00001B/5